> *"Everywhere I go, people tell me, 'Keep it country— don't change it.'"*
> —GEORGE STRAIT

From tiny Poteet, Texas, to country music superstardom . . .

From his first hit single, "Unwound," to his latest chart toppers, "Carrying Your Love with Me" and "Today My World Slipped Away," here is the up-to-the-minute biography of a legend at the top of his form.

"George Strait . . . may just be the finest country music performer since Hank Williams."
> —ANDREW VAUGHAN,
> *Who's Who in New Country Music*

"George Strait continues to get better and better."
> —CHET FLIPPO,
> *Billboard*

By Jo Sgammato
Published by Ballantine Books:

DREAM COME TRUE: The LeAnn Rimes Story
KEEPIN' IT COUNTRY: The George Strait Story

KEEPIN' IT COUNTRY

COUNTRY

The George Strait Story

Jo Sgammato

BALLANTINE BOOKS • NEW YORK

A Ballantine Book
Published by The Ballantine Publishing Group
Copyright © 1998 by Jo Sgammato

http://www.randomhouse.com

Library of Congress Catalog Card Number: 97-97149

ISBN 0-345-42425-5

Manufactured in the United States of America

First Edition: March 1998

10 9 8 7 6 5 4 3 2

For my parents,
Dominick and Mary Sgammato.
Thanks to you, tradition is important to me, too.

CONTENTS

CONTENTS

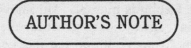

AUTHOR'S NOTE

When I came to Nashville for the first time in July of 1993, I heard a song on the radio that seemed to represent all that is wonderful about country music: a good story, a sense of humor, a catchy melody, and the voice of a great singer obviously enjoying himself.

The song was called "All My Ex's Live in Texas." Only later did I discover that it had been a huge hit for George Strait. By that time I was already one of his many fans.

Then Ballantine Books asked me to write a biography of George Strait. Fans were asking booksellers for a book about the country music superstar from the Lone Star State.

This welcome assignment gave me the opportunity to travel again through the great state of Texas: to San Antonio and the flat, magnificent ranch country of south Texas and to New Braunfels and San Marcos in the Hill Country. It's easy to see why George Strait loves his home state.

It's also easy to see why his fans love him.

Though he is modest and by all accounts a true gentleman, George Strait brings out the kind of adoration in fans usually reserved for performers who live for the spotlight.

And the feeling is mutual. "Through the years, the fans have always been great for me," George Strait says. "They've supported me, come to my shows, and bought my records. I've just tried to give them the best that I could do the whole time."

George Strait can already legitimately be called a legend and he's only in his mid-forties. He has been at the top for an amazing sixteen years in a business where, these days, people rarely last six.

During the 1980s and 1990s, Strait has racked up more number-one hits than anyone else in the country music scene, sold an amazing forty million albums, and won every award in the business. In an age of slick packaging and marketing of music, he has stayed true to his musical roots of traditional country music, honky tonk, and Western swing.

George Strait's fans know he's a private man and respect him for that. But they still want to know more about him. Although I've not met George Strait, I am now proud to be a bigger fan than ever before. I hope this book gives fans even more to celebrate about George Strait and that George Strait enjoys this tribute on behalf of all of us.

KEEPIN' IT COUNTRY

CHAPTER ONE

Startin' Out Country

On Wednesday evening, September 24, 1997, country music fans all over America were watching their TVs. The thirty-first annual Country Music Association Awards show was on, broadcasting live coast to coast from Nashville. Early in the show, beloved country singer Vince Gill, who was hosting the show for the sixth straight year, announced the third performer of the evening.

"Here is the great George Strait," he said, and the entire country music industry assembled in the Grand Ole Opry burst out cheering.

The tall, handsome country music superstar from Texas waved to the audience as he came onstage and took his microphone. Wearing blue jeans, brown boots, a white shirt, a mustard-colored jacket, and, of course, his trademark Resistol cowboy hat, he smiled broadly at his peers in the industry and the millions of fans in the home audience.

The catchy first few bars of his number-one hit single "Carrying Your Love with Me," from the album of the same name, made the audience smile back.

As he sang, Strait added even more country flourishes than were on the record and a distinctive yodel to the song. As usual when he performs, the women were screaming and the men were cheering. When the song was over, he smiled and bowed.

The audience gave him some of the most enthusiastic applause of the evening. The artists, songwriters, producers, and record-company executives in the Grand Ole Opry knew that without George Strait, it would be a different country music business for all of them.

Twenty years earlier, when he'd first come to Nashville, wearing his cowboy hat, singing traditional hard-core country music, George Strait was dismissed as "too country" and told to leave the hat back in Texas. Of course, now that he's sold forty million albums, he's considered the white-hatted hero from the West who turned the country music business around. And most of the "hat acts" that have followed admit that they owe their careers to him.

As predictable as the argument about the superiority of beef or pork ribs, the debate over "traditional" versus "pop-influenced" country music is again raging in Nashville. With country music once again big business, some people want to expand its appeal in order to "cross over" to a larger audience.

This is where George Strait came in. At the start of his career, he told an interviewer, "I want to reach the point where people hear my name and immediately think of real country music. I think what I'm doing is a little bit different from everything else that's out there on the radio . . . and I'd like to keep it that way."

He has definitely achieved that goal.

In a city accustomed to grand annual events involving country music's top stars and industry bigwigs, CMA Week, as it is called in Nashville, is the biggest event of them all.

For days, a stream of limousines had been rolling up and down Music Row—as the long avenues, smaller side streets, and aptly named Music Square and Music Circle are collectively known. The stars were out and about, making even more visits than usual to the office buildings and fine old-fashioned houses where the people of country music conduct their business.

Private parties, power lunches, celebrations between artists and the teams that made them stars were taking place at Nashville's finer restaurants. Nominees in each category were strutting their celebrated stuff, making the most of their status before the Wednesday night awards ceremony that would leave only one of them clutching the fourteen-inch bullet-shaped chunk of handblown glass that is the CMA trophy.

On Sunday, Garth Brooks, Clint Black, Toby Keith, Cledus "T." Judd, Rhett Akins, and Vince

Gill were among the stars at the Sprint Music Row Celebrity Golf Tournament.

LeAnn Rimes hosted the NationsBank Bowling Bash and Minnesota Fats Rack 'Em Up Billiards Tournament at Nashville's Hermitage Lanes on Monday evening. Country music's newest superstar wore a shirt printed with pink elephants along with a pair of ripped jeans. Moving to the beat of disco music and filling up on great food catered by the Hard Rock Café, the crowd had a wonderful time.

The proceeds of these events, as well as a tennis tournament hosted by Chely Wright, were to benefit the T. J. Martell Foundation for Leukemia, Cancer and AIDS Research.

Also on Monday night, ASCAP, the American Society of Composers, Authors and Publishers, held its annual black-tie awards dinner at the glittering Opryland Hotel. BMI, Broadcast Music Inc., followed with its gala event on Tuesday night. ASCAP and BMI are performing-rights agencies that collect and distribute income to songwriters and publishers for the public performance, particularly radio airplay, of their songs.

All day Wednesday, the artists who would be performing at the CMAs were out at the Grand Ole Opry, several miles east of the city, rehearsing for that evening's broadcast. The Country Music Association's thirtieth awards show, broadcast in October of 1996, had been the year's second-highest-rated variety entertainment special. Only the Oscars were seen by more people.

Founded in 1958, the Country Music Association was the first trade organization formed to promote any type of music. Providing a unity of purpose for the country music industry is its foremost goal. The CMA works to guide and enhance the development of country music throughout the world.

The CMA Awards show has been telecast for thirty of its thirty-one years. It has been broadcast live since 1969, when Johnny Cash set a record by winning five awards. In 1997, two artists each had five nominations, and at least on Wednesday during their rehearsals, the hope was that they would match Johnny Cash's achievement.

One of those artists was Deana Carter, a Nashville native whose debut album, *Did I Shave My Legs for This?*, had gone triple platinum, driven by the amazing hit single "Strawberry Wine."

The other artist to be honored with five CMA nominations was a Texas native whose sixteen years at the top had made him a legend. His career total of forty-two nominations was only one less than the all-time most-nominated performer, one of his musical heroes, Merle Haggard.

That artist was George Strait.

When the CMA nominations had been announced on August 5, Strait's name was on the list for Entertainer of the Year, Male Vocalist of the Year, and Album of the Year for *Carrying Your Love with Me*. In addition to making headlines with his five nominations, he made the record books. For the first time in more than twenty-five years, one artist had been nominated for *two* songs in the category Single of the Year.

One was "Carried Away," written by Steve Bogard and Jeff Stevens, from the *Blue Clear Sky* album. The other song was "One Night at a Time," written by Earl Bud Lee, Eddie Kilgallon, and Roger Cook, from Strait's latest album, *Carrying Your Love with Me*. (The CMAs include another category called Song of the Year, and the difference is that *single* is awarded to the artist, whereas *song* is awarded to the songwriter.)

The Country Music Association is proud of its three-ballot voting procedure. Among its seven thousand members are artists, executives, and members of the country music media. An accounting firm supervises the process, which begins, logically, when members choose the nominees.

Carrying Your Love with Me was nominated for Album of the Year along with two phenomenal platinum sellers: *Blue* by LeAnn Rimes and *Did I Shave My Legs for This?* by Deana Carter. *Everybody Knows* by Trisha Yearwood and *Everything I Love* by Alan Jackson rounded out the category.

Veteran singer and superstar Glen Campbell announced the award and, to the delight of the audience, handed the prize to Strait.

"Thank you very much. This really means a lot," Strait said, amid the cheers of the crowd. "I gotta thank Tony Brown, my producer, MCA Records, Bruce Hinton, everyone at MCA who supports me. Thanks to the great songwriters who wrote the songs for my album, thanks for giving your songs to me. . . . I really appreciate it."

For George Strait, an artist who always makes the music itself the centerpiece of his show, rather than glitzy showmanship or elaborate productions, Album of the Year is probably the most significant and gratifying award to win. To triumph over *Blue* and *Did I Shave My Legs*, either of which could have easily taken the prize, said a lot.

This was Strait's third Album of the Year honor. In 1996 he won with *Blue Clear Sky*. Back in 1985 he won for the first album he coproduced, the critically acclaimed *Does Fort Worth Ever Cross Your Mind*.

"You know that Album of the Year is pretty special," he said backstage. "The musicians we have in the studio, all the guys up for Musician of the Year, I've worked with on most of my albums. We have fun. I give them a lot of credit, they make it fun for me."

AND THE WINNER IS . . .

George Strait has sold almost forty million albums and won numerous top awards in his sixteen years at the top of the country music business. Here are some of the trophies keeping all his gold and platinum citations company.

COUNTRY MUSIC ASSOCIATION

MALE VOCALIST OF THE YEAR
1985

ALBUM OF THE YEAR
Awarded to the Artist and Record Company
Does Fort Worth Ever Cross Your Mind
George Strait/MCA Records
1985

MALE VOCALIST OF THE YEAR
1986

ENTERTAINER OF THE YEAR
1989

ENTERTAINER OF THE YEAR
1990

MALE VOCALIST OF THE YEAR
1996

ALBUM OF THE YEAR
Blue Clear Sky
George Strait/MCA Records
1996

SINGLE OF THE YEAR
Awarded to the Artist and Record Company
"Check Yes or No"

George Strait/MCA Records
1996

MALE VOCALIST OF THE YEAR
1997

ALBUM OF THE YEAR
Carrying Your Love with Me
George Strait/MCA Records
1997

ACADEMY OF COUNTRY MUSIC

TOP MALE VOCALIST
1984

TOP MALE VOCALIST
1985

ALBUM OF THE YEAR
Awarded to Artist/Producer/Record Company
Does Fort Worth Ever Cross Your Mind
George Strait/Produced by Jimmy Bowen and
George Strait/MCA Records
1985

TOP MALE VOCALIST
1988

ENTERTAINER OF THE YEAR
1989

TEX RITTER AWARD
Presented Occasionally for a Movie
with a Country Theme
Pure Country
1992

SINGLE RECORD OF THE YEAR
Awarded to Artist/Producer/Record Company
"Check Yes or No"
George Strait/Produced by Tony Brown and
George Strait/MCA Records
1995

SONG OF THE YEAR
Awarded to Composer/Publisher/Artist
"Check Yes or No"
Danny A. Wells, Dana Hunt Oglesby/John Juan
Music, Victoria Kay Music/George Strait
1995

TOP MALE VOCALIST
1996

ALBUM OF THE YEAR
Awarded to Artist/Producer/Record Company
Blue Clear Sky
George Strait/Produced by Tony Brown
and George Strait/MCA Records
1996

AMERICAN SOCIETY OF COMPOSERS, AUTHORS AND PUBLISHERS

VOICE OF MUSIC AWARD
1995

TNN/MUSIC CITY NEWS AWARDS

ALBUM OF THE YEAR
Lead On
1996

VIDEO OF THE YEAR
"Check Yes or No"
1996

SINGLE OF THE YEAR
"Check Yes or No"
1996

BILLBOARD

NEW MALE ALBUM ARTIST OF THE YEAR
1981

MALE SINGLES ARTIST OF THE YEAR
1983

MALE VOCALIST OF THE YEAR
1984

OVERALL TOP ARTIST
1986

TOP MALE ARTIST
1986

COUNTRY ARTIST OF THE YEAR
1987

COUNTRY ARTIST OF THE YEAR
1996

Faith Hill presented the Male Vocalist of the Year award. The nominees were Vince Gill, Alan Jackson, Collin Raye, Bryan White, and George Strait. Strait won Male Vocalist in 1985, 1986, and again in 1996.

She opened the envelope . . . and read Strait's name.

The audience was on its feet, in its first standing ovation of the evening.

"Thank you very much," he said. "This is unbelievable. I'm glad I got to come up here again because I forgot to thank all the fans. You're the most important people in this business. . . . Thanks also to my wife and son, who are here tonight and have supported me over the years."

Later he said, "This is pretty awesome."

George Strait and Garth Brooks are tied for second place on the CMA's all-time win list. Only Vince Gill with seventeen CMAs exceeds them. Earlier, Brooks had said that if the awards were given for true quality, they would all go to George Strait. "In my eyes," Garth said, "he's a superstar."

Strait was the only artist to take home two awards that night.

The gleaming skyscrapers, fancy hotels, shiny new Alamodome, and traditional Spanish-American architecture of San Antonio—all joined together by the dazzling Riverwalk along the San Antonio River—make it one of America's favorite cities. Driving south with San Antone in the rearview mirror, you begin to see the countryside almost immediately.

Poteet, Texas, is about twenty-five miles south of San Antonio on Highway 16. Just as the Texas Hill Country is about to turn flat, the sign for Poteet appears. Poteet, in Atascosa County, might as well be twenty-five thousand miles away from San Antonio, that's how small and rural it is. But everyone who loves music of any kind, and especially those who love country music, owes this little town a debt of gratitude. This is the place where George Strait was born on May 18, 1952.

George and his older brother, Buddy, are fourth-generation Texans in a state where pride of place is valued even more than the oil that gushes forth from the earth.

Though born in Poteet, he grew up about thirty miles to the southwest in Pearsall, the county seat of Frio County, near the Frio River. His father, John, was a junior-high-school math teacher and part-time rancher.

When George was in the fourth grade, his parents divorced, and the two brothers were raised by their father. "He just dedicated the rest of his whole life to raising my brother and me," Strait said. "And he very seldom even dated. He taught school and worked on the ranch. It was only after Buddy and I got out of the house that he cut loose and started having some fun again, and eventually remarried."

Pearsall, Texas, with a population of five thousand, is known as the largest peanut producer in the state. The town was founded as a stop on the railroad, which reached Pearsall on Independence Day, 1880. Town-lot sales began that day. Today, Pearsall has become a center for agriculture, ranching, and petroleum.

Life during the week consisted of school for all three Straits. In fact, both Buddy and George were students in their father's math classes. On the weekends they drove the forty miles down Route 85 into Big Wells, where John's father had a ranch. An hour from the Mexican border, Big Wells is in the Texas brush country, where, it is said, everything either stings, bites, or has thorns.

"About the time most young men were playing Little League baseball," Strait says, "I was learning to rope and ride."

Mountains and oceans may be dramatic in their beauty and celebrated more often than plain flatland, but the vast, open expanse of Texas brush country is nothing short of awesome. The sky really is as big as they say and it surrounds you, seeming to come all the way to the ground on a horizon that is a sliver of green. Asphalt is a rare sight, and dirt roads on either side lead into huge tracts of acreage. You can drive for miles and miles and see nothing but mesquite trees on either side of the road, rising from golden-brown earth known for its dryness. The oil pumps, small clusters of tanks, and pipeline stations remind you, as does the occasional smell of oil, that the earth here is rich in other ways.

Longhorn cattle, descendants of the Spanish cattle that had been brought to the area centuries earlier, roam the land along with the breeds of today: the red-bodied, white-faced Herefords and black Angus and the Santa Gertrudis, the first distinctly American breed of cattle. Sometimes the cattle get lost in the thickets of mesquite, dwarf oaks, and prickly-pear cactus.

All kinds of music was playing around him, but George Strait did not grow up in a musical home. Unlike many other country music stars, he wasn't a child with a passion to play or sing and he didn't have a parent or relative who instilled in him a driving urge to be a star. Instead, he seems to have absorbed the music in his surroundings in a more subtle way.

"I was interested in music in high school but it was more rock and roll," Strait says. "I mean, the Beatles were big then, so I was listening a lot to them and to a lot of other pop music at the time."

The music most a part of life in Texas at the time was honky tonk. With its danceable beats and songs of love and heartache, this is the music most people thought of, and many still think of, when you mentioned "country" music.

The prosperity of the late nineteenth and early twentieth centuries in Texas's cotton-growing country had come to an abrupt halt with the invasion of the boll weevil in the early 1920s and the Great Depression of the thirties. Prohibition prevented anyone from drinking alcohol, at least legally. But the bad times didn't last forever.

The Depression ended, Prohibition was repealed, and oil boomed in Texas. Plenty of oil workers with a few bucks in their pockets were available to patronize the many honky tonks that sprang up everywhere. Great music wasn't far behind.

Singers and players like Ernest Tubb, Floyd Tillman, and Lefty Frizell began a tradition of music that reflected the often harsh reality of life as it was lived by real people. Hank Williams, George Jones, and Merle Haggard carried on the tradition, singing of livin' and lovin' and workin' and tryin' to keep the faith in another tomorrow. All of these giants of country music could be heard on the radio during the years George Strait was growing up.

THE HEROES OF COUNTRY

LEFTY FRIZZELL, 1928–1975

Born in Corsicana, Texas, William Orville Frizzell grew up to become one of country music's most legendary artists and songwriters. He had a unique and innovative singing style and wrote classic songs that have influenced the careers of major country performers for decades. At one point, four of his songs simultaneously appeared in the top ten on the national country charts.

MERLE HAGGARD, 1937–

Called the "Poet of the Common Man," Merle Haggard writes and performs songs that tell the truth about the lives of ordinary people. Born in a converted boxcar in Bakersfield, California, he grew up in poverty and turmoil and, for a long time, lived the life of a hobo. He rose to stardom with songs like "Mama Tried," "Ramblin' Fever," "Workin' Man Blues," and "Okie from Muskogee."

GEORGE JONES, 1931–

Many consider George Jones the greatest country singer of all time. Born in Saratoga, Texas, he started working local shows in his teens and began recording in 1955. He went on to cut numerous hits, from the humorous "White Lightning" to the anguished "Window Up Above" to the classic "He Stopped Loving Her Today." Jones's honky tonk songs are part of country music's lifeblood.

FLOYD TILLMAN, 1914–

A songwriter, widely imitated vocal stylist, and instrumentalist in the best honky tonk tradition, Tillman was born in Oklahoma and raised in Texas. Throughout the 1930s, he paid his musical dues in honky tonks, bars, and roadhouses all over the Lone Star State. "It Makes No Difference Now," "I Love You So Much It Hurts," and "Slipping Around" are among the hundreds of songs he wrote.

HANK WILLIAMS, 1923–1953

If only one man can be said to represent the heart and soul of country music, it is the singer/songwriter Hank Williams. Born in rural Alabama and raised during the Depression, Williams began performing as the "Singing Kid." He died from illness and the ravages of alcoholism at the age of thirty. His immortal songs include "Lovesick Blues," "Your Cheatin' Heart," and "I'm So Lonesome I Could Cry."

Ranches in Big Wells and the surrounding towns are huge, often thousands of acres in size (although it is considered the height of rudeness to ask a Texan how much land he owns).

Texas is the place where the legend of the American cowboy began. Many of the skills and gear used on the ranch come from the vaqueros, the Mexican cowboys. (The word *buckaroo* is a loose translation of "vaquero.")

Cowboys were herding cattle for centuries before fences made of barbed wire came along in 1874. The thick suede chaps that cowboys wore over their pants saved their legs from the thorny brush. The bridles and saddles used on the horses, as well as the spurs to move them onward, all came from the Mexican cowboys. The branding of cattle also began when the Spanish introduced the longhorn cattle into what was then northern Mexico.

Today's ranchers have Jeeps, helicopters, and telephones at their disposal, but there is still no substitute for the cowboy on his trusted horse, riding the fields and roping in the stubborn steer who choose to stray.

What is unique to the U.S.A. is the cowboy hat, chosen by the Texas cowboys themselves. The wide-brimmed hat offered shade from the unrelenting sun and protection from rain and hail. It could also be used as an emergency water bucket. The ten-gallon hat didn't carry ten gallons of water, but after ten trips to the stream, it was usually time to buy a new one.

This is the land where George Strait's roots run deep. The life he led was defined by the rhythm of operating a ranch, the enjoyment of music in honky tonks and other social halls and saloons, and church on Sundays. The Strait family, devout Baptists, maintained a religious atmosphere in their lives and homes.

"We're all Baptists," Strait says, "and my father always told me that the Lord would tell me what he wanted me to do with my life and I kind of believe that's true. So I didn't worry about it much."

George Strait played the cornet in junior high. In high school he played drums and sang in garage bands. Like their counterparts all over America, Strait's first bands played songs like "Gloria" and "Louie Louie."

"No one, including myself, could really play guitar," Strait says.

In 1970, he graduated with honors from Pearsall High School. He went up to San Marcos, north of San Antone, to Southwest Texas State University.

After one semester he left and eloped to Mexico with his high-school sweetheart, Norma. Their parents gave them a formal wedding soon after they returned.

John Strait had retired from teaching and taken over the family's large ranch full-time. He wanted his son to become a rancher, too. George agreed to do so, but first he wanted to do his bit for his country in the military. Joining the army in 1971, he was stationed in Hawaii at Schofield

Barracks. He was assigned to work in the payroll department.

"I don't know how I managed Hawaii," he said later. "You know, when you go in you fill out one of those 'dream sheets' you call 'em? They ask for overseas duty and stateside duty and you put down what you want. I put down Hawaii. What the hell, you can try it. . . . And I put down Fort Carson, Colorado, for stateside duty. Man, I got my orders to go to Hawaii, I just could not believe it!"

The lushly beautiful Hawaiian islands with year-round perfect weather and sunsets to die for was a wonderful place for the newly wed Norma and George Strait to spend the first few years of their marriage.

While he was there George Strait heard Merle Haggard's *Tribute to the Best Damn Fiddle Player in the World (or My Salute to Bob Wills)*. By this time, his musical tastes had changed from the Beatles and rock and roll.

The upbeat, spirited dance-hall music known as Western swing was hugely popular in the thirties, forties, and fifties. The creation of Bob Wills, Western swing was a mix of early country western, blues, New Orleans jazz, folk fiddle, and the big band sounds of Count Basie, Benny Goodman, and Glenn Miller. Wills and his Western swing sound combined drums, two or three fiddles, electric and steel guitars, saxophones, trumpets, and piano in a whole new way.

Bob Wills is thought by many to be one of the most influential artists in country music, although he didn't even consider himself a country musician. Part American Indian, he made an enormous contribution to the changing American culture of the early and mid-twentieth century by bringing black and white music together and bringing country music to the cities. One of his most famous hits was "San Antonio Rose."

"Bob Wills and the Texas Playboys are simply the best band that ever was," George Strait has said. They certainly became the primary influence on him, and his high regard for them is reflected in every one of his albums.

BOB WILLS

Bob Wills will always be known for creating a uniquely American music combining everything from Mexican mariachi to German polkas, from the blues to cowboy music, and from Dixieland jazz to fiddle hoedowns.

The oldest of ten children, he was born James Robert Wills in 1905 in Kosse, Texas, southeast of Fort Worth. The family was poor—they picked cotton alongside their black neighbors—but rich in musical talent. Both of Wills's grandfathers, five of his aunts, and nine of his uncles played the fiddle.

Wills's first instrument was the mandolin, but he played fiddle at square dances and had his first professional engagement in the Texas Panhandle at the age of ten. Later, he went to New Mexico, where he learned traditional Mexican music, and to Fort Worth, where he performed fiddle tunes, tricks, and dance routines in a medicine show.

In the early 1930s, he formed his first group. Since they played to advertise Light Crust Flour on the radio, they called themselves the Light Crust Doughboys. By 1933, Wills called the band Bob Wills and the Texas Playboys, with singer Tommy Duncan in the lead. Soon they were making records and becoming wildly popular with audiences who loved Wills's wisecracks, musical experiments, and just plain outrageousness.

With all the instruments Wills wanted to include, the band was up to eighteen pieces by 1940. From Texas to Oklahoma to California, Bob Wills and the Texas Playboys were superstars. They were featured in a number of Hollywood movies and were regulars in Las Vegas. Over the years, scores of musicians played with Bob Wills, on the road and on his recording sessions.

Favorite hits include "Home in San Antone," "Milkcow Blues," "Ida Red," "Cherokee Maiden," "Take Me Back to Tulsa," "Big Ball's in Cowtown," "Corinna, Corinna," "Faded

Love," and "Steel Guitar Rag." "San Antonio Rose" was a million-selling song both for Wills and for Bing Crosby.

When Bob Wills and the Texas Playboys played in Nashville at the Grand Ole Opry in 1940, they wore cowboy hats and boots and bolo ties. Some say that soon afterward, many Nashville artists stopped wearing their flannel shirts and overalls and imitated the Texas Playboys' look.

Bob Wills brought some rock-and-roll songs into the band's repertoire in the fifties and sixties. He had always had some health problems, and though they worsened in these decades, he continued to tour and record. In 1968, he was inducted into the Country Music Hall of Fame. Later he was honored by Governor Preston Smith and the state of Texas for his contribution to American music. The next day he suffered a stroke.

Bob Wills died in 1975. In 1982 Merle Haggard, one of his biggest fans, recorded an album called *Tribute to the Best Damn Fiddle Player in the World (or My Salute to Bob Wills)*. Haggard received Bob's fiddle as a gift, which he still plays onstage.

In 1991, Rhino Records released *Bob Wills and His Texas Playboys Anthology (1935–1973)*. The thirty-two-track set retraces Wills's recording career from the first Texas Playboys sessions in 1935 to his 1973 farewell appearance with the Playboys on the album *For the Last Time*.

"I started getting interested in country music shortly after my senior year in high school," George Strait said. "And once I got interested in country, I just fell in love with it." That music had gotten under his skin without his even knowing it.

While in Hawaii, George bought a six-string guitar, a Hank Williams songbook, and sheet music by George Jones, Bob Wills, and Merle Haggard. He taught himself to play guitar.

He also got a very lucky break. After all, how many base commanders in the army decide to form a band for the entertainment of the officers and enlisted personnel? George Strait's base commander did just that, and when Strait auditioned to be the lead singer in the country band, he got the gig. For the next two years he honed his musical skills, learning to feel comfortable playing for an audience. It got so he didn't even have to wear a uniform for the last two years of his service and performed in his civilian clothes and his cowboy hat.

"I always knew I wanted to be a singer, but it wasn't until I ended up in Hawaii that I really got serious about it," he said.

The band played at numerous parties and official functions. "It gave me the time I needed to learn all about playing dates, because it's, you know, a scary thing to do that at first," Strait said.

While Norma and George Strait were in Hawaii, their daughter, Jenifer, was born, and the family stayed in the beautiful islands after Strait left the service. But it was difficult to make a living there and the cost of living was high. They decided to return home after six months.

Back in San Marcos in 1975, George reenrolled in Southwest Texas State University. Famed Texan and former U.S. President Lyndon Johnson is among the school's graduates. George studied agriculture on the GI Bill. He had decided against going after a degree in music. "I wasn't all that interested in learnin' to read music," he said. "And the type of voice lessons they give you, well, they want to teach you to sing opera. I just wasn't interested."

A typical college town in the Texas Hill Country, San Marcos is lush and green, with the San Marcos River running right through its center. Up on a hill overlooking the town is the university. Numerous small apartment complexes can be found near the school.

After two years with the army-base band in Hawaii, George Strait was now a singer in search of a new band. He placed an ad on a bulletin board and got another lucky break: a band called Stoney Ridge was looking for a new lead singer. Though he showed up for his audition wearing a Hawaiian shell necklace and sporting long hair and a deep tan, there was little doubt in the band's mind after hearing him that George Strait was an authentic country singer. And a darned good one at that.

Country music of the mid 1970s is known for its openness to pop music influences: lots of strings, "big" orchestrations, and smooth, polished vocals. Typical of the trend, in 1974, Australian pop singer Olivia Newton-John had won Female Vocalist of the Year at the Country Music Association Awards. She was known for such pop-country blends as "If You Love Me (Let Me Know)," "I Honestly Love You," and "Have You Never Been Mellow?" and the big hit from the movie *Grease*, "Hopelessly Devoted to You." In 1975, the late pop singer John Denver crossed over into country and won the CMA Award for Entertainer of the Year. He had huge hits with "Take Me Home, Country Roads" and "Thank God I'm a Country Boy." His success also indicated the presence of a younger market for country music that hadn't yet been tapped.

In retrospect, it seems in some ways the worst time to have tried to form a traditional country band. But George Strait and his new band knew right from the start that they were going to be country all the way. They named themselves the Ace in the Hole Band.

Bass player Terry Hale, steel guitarist Mike Daily, lead guitarist Ron Cabal, and drummer Tommy Foote were also students at Southwest Texas State University. At twenty-three years old,

George was the oldest member of the group and the only one who was married and a father.

On October 14, 1975, the Ace in the Hole Band had their first show at the Cheatham Street Warehouse on the corner of Guadalupe and Cheatham streets, next to the railroad tracks in San Marcos. Like all college towns, especially in the 1970s when the drinking age was eighteen, San Marcos had plenty of bars. But the Cheatham Street Warehouse was special. So out, it was in; so off-the-beaten-track, it was especially hip to go there.

It could hardly even be called a building. With its corrugated metal exterior, it looked like a small tin barn or a farm shed built several feet off the ground with a plywood floor. The beer was cheap and the music was loud. Willie Nelson and many others had played there.

The audience was made up of a handful of people, mostly friends of the band who were on the guest list. They weren't getting rich that night.

The Ace in the Hole Band played their hearts out while George Strait stood up front and sang. The set was one hundred percent, hard-core country, with some honky tonk and Western swing thrown in. "I discovered in college that country music could be fun by adding some swing to it," Strait said.

The audience loved it. Did they know they were watching history in the making?

Whether they did or not, the Ace in the Hole Band became a regular feature at the Cheatham

Street Warehouse. Every Wednesday night the cover charge was fifty cents for men. Ladies were admitted free. Sometimes only ten or fifteen people were in the audience.

George Strait had enjoyed singing in an army country music band in Hawaii. Now he was back in his home state, singing the music he'd been raised with, playing in a band he believed in. It had to be an incredible high. It certainly helped to cement his decision to pursue a career choosing the songs he loved, singing them the best he knew how, and getting paid for it.

"Everything was always secondary to music," he said. "Music was always what I wanted to do."

George Strait and the Ace in the Hole Band, like a lot of aspiring musicians, attended college by day and worked the bars at night. They played wherever they could find a gig in San Marcos and the surrounding area. Sometimes, between the five of them, they made a whole two hundred and fifty dollars a night!

At the time, there was a club in San Marcos called the Prairie Rose, owned by Erv Woolsey, from Houston, Texas. Woolsey had worked in radio promotion for Decca and a few other companies in the late sixties and early seventies. He owned the Prairie Rose for only about a year before going to Nashville to head up country music promotion for MCA Records.

"When I first heard George sing," Woolsey says, "I was standing in the back of the club with my back to him. When I heard him crank up, I just had to turn around and see who was singing. I knew right away that he was a great singer."

It would turn out to be very lucky for Erv Woolsey and for George Strait that their paths had crossed in San Marcos, Texas, in 1975.

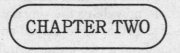

CHAPTER TWO

Travelin' Texas

Anyone who likes music loves the Beatles. Everyone who appreciates anything about the art of singing is a Frank Sinatra fan. For sheer delight in entertaining and in pumping out great sound, few can compare with Ray Charles.

Back in the 1970s, George Strait liked music as much as anyone, knew more about singing than most of us, and had already become entranced with the thrill of standing on a stage giving an audience a great show. So, one could say, he had even more reasons than the rest of us to admire The Beatles, Frank Sinatra, and Ray Charles.

But when it came to the music Strait wanted to sing and share with his own audiences in Texas, there was no doubt that it would not resemble that of these three legends. George Strait and the Ace in the Hole Band were, quite simply, keepin' it country. And the San Antonio area was loving it, most of the time.

Later, George told Mark McEwen of *CBS This Morning*, "Well, San Antonio is a great place to hear good music. There's a lot of clubs and places to go and hear live music. . . . I think a lot of people cut their teeth on these little honky tonks around this area . . . I know that's the way it was for me."

The Ace in the Hole Band played anyplace they could within about a two-hundred-mile radius of San Marcos. Roadhouses and honky tonks, dance halls and chili festivals, weddings and fraternity parties—anywhere folks gathered together to hear music and have a good time.

Looking back, Strait said, "You remember little things like back when you were carrying equipment around [in] the back of a pickup, and traveling around four in a cab. You're trying to do a show like ninety or a hundred, two hundred miles away. And packin' back up, carrying equipment out, loading it up, and going back home the same night."

It's the way a lot of bands paid their dues, building up a local audience and sharpening their skills, whether singing or playing their instruments. It's how you learn what the audiences like and what kind of an artist you ultimately want to be.

"I've always done other people's material," Strait said. "In the old days, that's all I did. I guess that's how I developed my style—by doing other people's material. When you are out there doing a four-hour club date and you're singing George Jones and Merle Haggard, that's what people want you to sound like. I don't do that anymore, but I think that helped."

The music that the Ace in the Hole Band loved

best was Western swing. "Back then, we could do two or three hours of solid swing," he said. "That was our thing. That's what we liked to play."

In hindsight, it was the start of a great career. At the time, however, "We were just a local band that never got much publicity. I mean, why should it have? We were just plugging around in the bars and honky tonks."

From College Station to Del Rio, Texas, folks came to hear George Strait and the Ace in the Hole Band play in bars and smoky ramshackle honky tonks with names like the Ramblin' Rose.

As time went on and the band became more popular in the San Antonio area, they continued to refuse to play anything but traditional country. They would just play, with barely a break between songs so that people wouldn't yell out requests for songs the band didn't want to play. Sticking to the music they liked lost them some gigs, but they chalked it up as the price of keepin' it country.

Mike Daily, the Ace in the Hole Band's steel guitar player, said, "We were never a Top 40 band. Never were. A lot of bands at that time were playing Top 40 and . . . they would do a lot of rock and roll in their sets. And we just never did that." Strait echoed the idea. "There were some clubs we never did play because of that. We wouldn't play Top 40 and we didn't break into a rock-and-roll song now and then, like a lot of bands thought they had to do. We just never did do it; we weren't going to do it. Still don't. It's not what we're going to do."

In the entertainment climate of the 1970s, when rock was hot and even country was influenced by pop, sticking to the traditional sounds of honky tonk and Western swing was a downright rebellious act.

Some gigs were better than others. In 1976, at the World's Largest Chili Cookoff—known as the Chilympiad—George Strait and the Ace in the Hole Band earned free passes for the big evening concert. Playing on that Saturday night were some of the original Texas Playboys, Leon Rausch, Leon McAuliffe, Joe Ferguson, Al Strickland, and Smoky Dacus. For Strait, meeting some of the players behind the late, great Bob Wills was a true thrill.

The folks who'd been eating chili all day were truly fired up! George Strait and the Ace in the Hole Band were a big hit, and were invited back again and again to play the Chilympiad. They were also hired on the spot to open up for the Texas Playboys on several shows.

The first time they opened a show for the Texas Playboys, the Ace in the Hole Band played their favorite Bob Wills music in the set. This turned out to be a little embarrassing when the Texas Playboys came out onstage and proceeded to play all the same songs! That taught Strait and the band a lesson. Still, they were lucky enough to be invited to play with the Playboys again.

When the Ace in the Hole Band played in Pearsall, Texas, they were booked as George Strait and the Ace in the Hole Band. It was George's hometown, and putting his name up front brought everyone out to hear them.

In the late seventies, George Strait and his Ace in the Hole Band played frequently at Gruene Hall in New Braunfels, Texas, about thirty miles north of San Antonio. The first settlers in the area were German farmers who arrived in the mid-1840s, drawn by the rich and fertile farmland in the rolling hills.

Among those immigrants who traveled halfway across America after arriving at the famous entry port of Ellis Island in New York City were Ernst Gruene (pronounced "Green") and his bride, Antoinette. In 1862, because acreage was no longer available in New Braunfels, Ernst and his two sons bought land in a community nearby.

By 1870, cotton was a big cash crop, and Ernst's son Henry advertised his need for sharecroppers. Soon twenty to thirty families occupied his land. In 1878, he established the first mercantile store in a white frame building on the main stage road from San Antonio to Austin on the banks of the Guadalupe River.

In the 1880s, Gruene built a dance hall and saloon. Gruene Hall provided entertainment for the tenants and surrounding farmers and was the center of the community's social life. Gruene built his own home, expanded it with Victorian galleries on three sides, and built other brick and frame homes. The town prospered for many years.

In 1925 and 1929, economic disaster struck with the boll weevil and the Great Depression. The Gruene family kept the mercantile store open and extended credit to farmers. Soon, though, this became impossible. The store closed and the town became a ghost town. In the mid 1970s, much of the Gruene estate was sold, but the historic value of the buildings caused them to be placed on the National Register of Historic Places.

"We would play Gruene Hall and our share of the door would be fifteen hundred dollars," lead guitarist Ron Cabal said. "We'd split it up and make three hundred a man for one night, which was great back then."

Believed to be the oldest dance hall in Texas, Gruene Hall, a big, open space with a peaked roof, is a landmark in Texas musical history. Signs all around the walls—a few neon, mostly old metal ones—advertise old businesses, from the Main Plaza Service Station to the Blue Bonnett Cleaners & Tailors. Screens on three sides and lots of ceiling fans provide natural air-conditioning.

The stage is set back in the wall, with the dance floor in front of it. Men in their striped shirts and white hats lead their wives and girlfriends, who are often dressed in the same colors or similar outfits, around the dance floor. At many long tables and benches, others sit and enjoy the music. On one side two pool tables can be seen, and outside, picnic tables line the big yard.

Such Texas stars as Lyle Lovett and Hank Ketchum also got their start in Gruene Hall. Near the entrance, their framed, autographed photos hang among hundreds of others, including great shots of Jimmie Dale Gilmore, Nanci Griffith, Michael Martin Murphy, the Texas Tornadoes, the late Townes Van Zandt, and Jerry Jeff Walker.

George Strait wrote on his photo, "To Pat, MJ and Nannette. Thanks for all the unforgettable nights at Gruene. We'll have many more, I'm sure. George Strait."

People who saw George Strait and the Ace in the Hole Band playing at Gruene Hall and other clubs in Texas in the late 1970s say he was amazing onstage, always connecting with the audience in an intimate way. They also say that offstage he was shy and quiet, staying to himself or staying close to his wife or family members. The women hanging around to see if the good-looking lead singer was available learned quickly, and to their disappointment, that he was a married man.

Today's audiences who see George Strait in huge arenas can only envy those lucky enough to have seen him in places like the Cheatham Street Warehouse, the Prairie Rose, or Gruene Hall.

Ray Benson and the Texas band Asleep at the Wheel are also famous for their devotion to

Western swing. They became aware of George Strait in 1978.

"We were playing at Gruene Hall," Benson says. "I was sitting on the bus listening to the opening band who was doing all the Texas dance-hall standards, and to my delight some old Western swing numbers. The lead singer had a great voice; but I couldn't see him, and when I asked who the band was, they said, 'Ace in the Hole.' Well, we played the show, and I didn't think about the opening act much until a number of months later when this record came out called 'Unwound.' The guy's name was George Strait, and my friend said, 'He's that guy in the Ace in the Hole band.' "

ASLEEP AT THE WHEEL

"Not only has George Strait racked up more number-one songs than I can recall, he has helped to revive and revitalize Bob Wills and Western swing music and reinvent the singing cowboy for the modern age."

—Ray Benson, lead singer,
Asleep at the Wheel

Ray Benson ought to know. He and his band turned to Western swing in 1971 when they felt an element of blues and jazz was missing from their country sound.

Asleep at the Wheel, formed in 1970, consisted at first of Ray Benson, Leroy Preston, Lucky Oceans, and Chris O'Connell. They started out rehearsing on a farm in Paw Paw, West Virginia, playing a lot of Merle Haggard, Hank Williams, and country songs by other writers. They moved to San Francisco in 1971 and added a jazz pianist, Floyd Domino.

Like George Strait, they were influenced by Merle Haggard's *A Tribute to the Best Damn Fiddle Player in the World (or My Salute to Bob Wills)*. The Western swing sounds Bob Wills had pioneered with his huge band ignited the musical imagination of Asleep at the Wheel. According to Ray Benson, once the band worked up a few Bob Wills tunes to include in their set, "It was love at first hearing." They've been known for their Western swing music ever since.

After recording their first album, *Comin' Right at Ya*, in 1973, the band decided to relocate to Austin, Texas, at the urging of Willie Nelson. They have remained there to this day. Their first top-ten hit was called "The Letter That Johnny Walker Red."

Through the late seventies, the band had a few more albums and several hit singles, including "Route 66" and "Miles and Miles of Texas." In 1977, they were named the Academy of Country Music's Best Touring Band.

The following year they won a Grammy Award for Best Country Instrumental Performance for "One O'Clock Jump."

In the 1980s, Asleep at the Wheel received two more Grammy Awards for the songs "String of Pars" and "Sugarfoot Rag." The band was also a favorite on college campuses. In 1990, they had a hit with Ronnie Dunn's "Boot Scootin' Boogie."

Asleep at the Wheel's most acclaimed album was their 1993 *Tribute to the Music of Bob Wills and the Texas Playboys*.

Over the years almost eighty different musicians have been part of Asleep at the Wheel, always under the steady leadership of Ray Benson. Their Western swing sound is the signature of a classic American band.

In 1976, George Strait and the Ace in the Hole Band got an opportunity any band would jump at: the chance to record some singles that could perhaps get them some radio play and exposure to a larger audience.

In 1958, country legend H. W. "Pappy" Daily, who had managed one of George Strait's idols, country superstar George Jones, for twenty years, founded the label D Records in Houston, and recorded Willie Nelson's first 45s and Claude Gray's 1960 hit version of Nelson's "Family Bible."

By 1975, the operation was in the hands of Bud and Don Daily, Pappy's sons. Don Daily is the father of Ace in the Hole steel guitarist Mike Daily.

"I encouraged them to come in and make a record," Don Daily said, "and they thought, well, they could use it to book some dances, using it for a promo copy. . . . We had a few small radio stations play it. That was about it."

They made the record in Doggett's Recording Studio, an old house on Studemont Street that had been converted into a studio. In 1978 and 1979, they returned to the studio to do what eventually became a total of eight songs. Three of these songs were written by George Strait: "I Just Can't Go on Dying Like This," "(That Don't Change) The Way I Feel About You," and "I Don't Want to Talk It Over Anymore." These are three of only four George Strait compositions ever recorded.

No doubt the experience of being in the studio was valuable to George and the other members of the Ace in the Hole Band. Over the course of the three years in which they made the records, their sound developed and each recording was better than the last.

Producer Don Daily remembers Strait as "self-confident but very shy. Just got up there and sang real sincere. Wasn't shy about gettin' up to the microphone and singing, but he just didn't have a lot to say."

The songs didn't go anywhere for a number of reasons, mostly because a small label like D Records couldn't really compete for radio play with bigger stars from the larger labels.

As to his songwriting, Strait says, "I tried to write 'em like what I thought was a good country song. Of course, we were proud of 'em. But I mean when you listen to 'em now, you can tell how rough they were. . . . In reality there wasn't a lot of hope for 'em to be . . . commercial successes.

"Finally, my big goal became getting a record company to sign me to a contract," Strait says. "That's every singer's dream out there."

Nashville was the place to go to make that dream come true, and George Strait had a great opportunity in 1977. Texas songwriter Darryl Staedtler had come to Austin after spending more than a decade in Nashville, where he'd written several successful songs. Staedtler needed a singer to record some demos of new songs.

The need for demos in Nashville works to everyone's benefit. A songwriter needs a good singer to record a taped version of the music and lyrics so that the songs can be heard by artists looking for new material. Singers need good songs to sing to showcase their voices and have material to play for record-company executives, producers, and A&R (artist and repertoire) people. Musicians and backup singers can make a decent living working demo sessions until they get hired as regular band members or, in some cases, get their own careers going.

Usually it is the music publishers, the individuals or companies who own the publishing rights to the songs, who pay the musicians and pay for the studio time, including the fees for the recording engineers. Publishers stand to make a lot of money if a song is recorded for an album by even a middle-level artist. Songs that become hit singles for big artists mean a fortune in income for publishers as well as for the writers.

George Strait, Darryl Staedtler, and Kent Finlay, the owner of the Cheatham Street Warehouse, hit the road for the drive from San Antonio and Austin to the mecca that beckons all country musicians, Nashville, Tennessee. They drove all night long.

Strait and his buddies stayed at the Hall of Fame Motor Inn on Division Street behind the Country Music Hall of Fame and Museum, just at the edge of Music Row, whose converted houses are home to many management companies, public-relations firms, and music publishers. Typically, the reception area is in the entry foyer and the offices are what were once living rooms and dining rooms. These houses create a very pleasant atmosphere in which to do the business of music.

Music Row also boasts numerous recording studios. It was in one of these that Strait worked with the studio musicians—including fiddle players Johnny Gimble and Buddy Spicher, and Weldon Myrick on steel—to record six songs by Darryl Staedtler. One of the songs was "80 Proof Bottle of Tear Stopper."

After the demo tapes were finished, the next step was to get them heard by record-label executives with the power to sign George Strait to a deal. This is another hurdle musicians need to jump. Every record company receives hundreds and hundreds of tapes every month from aspiring artists. Producers, engineers, artist managers, publicists—anyone connected even in the most remote way to the music business—are always being told about a great artist or group they need to listen to.

So even to get his demos listened to by a few labels was a big accomplishment for the handsome young man with the high hopes from San Antonio, Texas. That the songs actually got heard was good news.

The bad news was what all the listeners said: "too country."

That's what Nashville thought, but back in Texas, the Ace in the Hole Band was drawing large crowds. It was great that they were local favorites, but it didn't look like they were going to go any farther than that.

"We were a great Texas bar band," says Tom Foote, who was the Ace in the Hole drummer and is now the band's road manager. "George had the voice, he had the looks, and he was always focused. I saw the band as a way to keep from getting a job and a way to meet girls. George saw it as the future."

But it was a future that was harder and harder to hold on to. In 1979, Nashville was still cranking out pop-influenced music, and the lines between pop and country were being crossed over more often than a busy street.

Country singers were hitting pop charts, pop singers were showing up on country charts, and even Hollywood was getting into the act. Movies starring country singers were becoming hits, as were the soundtracks from these movies.

The old guard of country music, those who had made it big in the previous decades, were finding their record sales declining each year. The giants like Johnny Cash, Loretta Lynn, Waylon Jennings, and Conway Twitty were no longer riding high.

Being called "too country" when that was the only kind of music he really wanted to sing was a little discouraging for George Strait. He had a wife and young daughter to support. He also had a strong work ethic.

In 1979, George Strait graduated from college with his BA degree in agriculture. "I got a job managing the Hart Ranch in Martindale, Texas," he says. "We had about a thousand head of cattle on it, and I was responsible for everything."

Being a ranch manager involved backbreaking labor and hours on horseback searching for stray calves.

Strait said in an interview with the Nashville *Tennessean*, "I was just doing the ranching to supplement my income a little bit, you know. 'Course, if my career was to end tomorrow, I'd probably go back and do it again because I really liked it, but it sure is hard. I miss the fun parts, the roping and stuff like that, but I don't miss building fences."

THE ORIGINAL SINGING COWBOY
GENE AUTRY 1907–

Like the original singing cowboy, Gene
Autry, George Strait hails from Texas.

The man who paved the way for almost
every country music singer and entertainer,
Gene Autry recently celebrated his ninetieth
birthday. His Western songs, heard on the radio and in the movies, where he set box-office
records, made him the first country and western
songwriter and performer to gain worldwide
acclaim.

Born in Tioga, Texas, Autry was working in
the telegraph office at the Chelsea, Oklahoma,
train station when Will Rogers came in one day
to dispatch his column. Rogers "told me to get
myself a job in radio," Autry says. Over the
years, he went on to make six hundred and
thirty-five recordings, selling more than sixty-
five million records, including "That Silver-
Haired Daddy of Mine," the first gold record in
history.

Autry introduced singing-cowboy films to
America with *Tumbling Tumbleweeds* in 1935.
He went on to make ninety-one other films and
became a top cowboy box-office star. Astride
his horse Champion, "Wonder Horse of the
West," he always found time between saving
the West from the bad guys to break into a

tune. Kids worshiped him, and he created his "Cowboy Code" in 1940, the same year his *Melody Ranch* was launched on CBS radio.

After serving in the army from 1942 to 1946, he resumed his career, piloting his own twin-engine Beechcraft to rodeos and stage shows. In 1949, Autry recorded "Rudolph the Red-Nosed Reindeer," the third-best-selling single of all time. *The Gene Autry Show* debuted on CBS in 1950, after which the star produced two other cowboy shows, *Annie Oakley* and *Buffalo Bill Jr.*

Autry retired from acting in 1962. In 1969, he was inducted into the Country Music Hall of Fame. During the 1980s, he hosted The Nashville Network's *Melody Ranch Theatre*, which showcased his feature films. In 1987, he received his fifth star on the Hollywood Walk of Fame, the only celebrity with five.

In 1993, Gene Autry's *Back in the Saddle Again* went platinum for the second time since its release in 1939 when it was included on the soundtrack of *Sleepless in Seattle*.

It was becoming a weary time for George Strait. He started his workday at sunrise and got his second wind at sundown, when it was time to get cleaned up, change his clothes, and go out to perform at bars, dance halls, and county fairs. It wasn't over until the bars closed.

Ron Cabal says George never slowed down. "He would have laryngitis where he couldn't talk but he would still be able to sing perfectly," Cabal says. "We only had to cancel two weeks in the whole eight years I was with Ace, when George had pneumonia."

"I wasn't getting any younger and I had to find something," Strait says. "I had a family to support and we were getting behind. We were struggling." And now Norma was expecting their second child.

"I was twenty-seven years old," he says. "I'd been playing for six or seven years, and I was beginning to think I just wasn't good enough and maybe ought to try something else. I gave my band notice and signed up for a full-time job with this outfit in Uvalde, Texas, that designed cattle pens. But a week before I was to report for the job, I realized I just couldn't do it. And I decided to give it one more year."

The Ace in the Hole Band had stayed with him for five years, though he couldn't get a deal with any national record label. Their loyalty and devotion to the music was matched by the loyalty and support of George's wife. Although Norma was looking forward to the new house and the steady salary that would come with the job in Uvalde, she also wanted her husband to be happy.

"He had a look in his eyes, he'd been impossible to get along with since he'd decided to quit playing, and I knew he couldn't be happy if he didn't try to make it," she said. "George was moping around the house so much I couldn't stand it. I figured I didn't want to live in Uvalde with him like that, so we talked about his hopes in music. I wanted him to give it one more chance."

In 1980, two things happened that had nothing to do with George Strait and the Ace in the Hole band but that profoundly affected their future.

One was the release of the movie *Coal Miner's Daughter*, which brought the life of one of country music's greatest stars, Loretta Lynn, to theaters all over America. Starring Sissy Spacek as Loretta, it became a box-office hit. More important, at least as far as the music business was concerned, the soundtrack of the film became a top-twenty hit. In addition, it made the music of another country queen, Patsy Cline, popular again.

The second was also a movie, *Urban Cowboy*, which followed the adventures of a young Texas farmer, played by John Travolta, who moves to Houston to work in an oil refinery. Once he arrives in the city, he becomes a regular at a honky tonk bar—the real-life Gilley's in Pasadena, Texas— where he and his friends drink, party, flirt with women, and ride mechanical bulls. Travolta falls in love with Debra Winger, with whom he has a stormy romance. Suddenly, girls all over the country were imitating Debra Winger, wearing cowboy hats and rocking around on a mechanical bull, while guys were sporting tight jeans, big belt buckles, and boots like John Travolta.

But the real impact of the film on the country music business was the result of its hugely successful soundtrack. Most of the artists featured on the album were decidedly not country. Jimmy Buffet, Joe Walsh, Dan Fogelberg, and Bob Seeger and the Silver Bullet Band were joined by Bonnie Raitt, Kenny Rogers, the Charlie Daniels Band, Linda Rondstadt, and Boz Scaggs. The success of the *Urban Cowboy* soundtrack reinforced the notion that crossing over into pop sounds was the way for country music to go.

Meanwhile, out in Texas and other parts of the Southwest, Michael Martin Murphy was gaining fame as the "Cosmic Cowboy." Willie Nelson was doing what some were calling "Redneck Rock." In Bakersfield, California, a new rockin' country sound all its own was drawing big crowds.

It was in this changed climate that George Strait, a *real* cowboy, a Texas native devoted to *real* old-fashioned country, *real* honky tonk, and *real* Western swing music, decided to give show business one last try.

Erv Woolsey, the onetime owner of the Prairie Rose club in San Marcos, was now a vice president at MCA Records in Nashville. According to Strait, "I called Erv and said, 'Isn't there some producer up there in Nashville that you can get to do a session on me?' I said I'd pay for it," he remembers. "I just wanted to get up to Nashville and do something once and for all. I felt like I was spinning my wheels."

Erv put Strait together with producer Blake Mevis. They recorded some more demos, including Darryl Staedtler's "Blame It on Mexico," and "Nobody in His Right Mind Would've Left Her" by Dean Dillon. Although MCA's A&R director, Ron Chancey, and label head Jim Fogelsong liked the demos, their verdict was still "too country."

"I went home with my tail between my legs," Strait said. "I was all upset and discouraged. . . . I was beginning to have doubts about myself. I was wonderin' whether I was really good enough to make it—whether I was just bein' foolish, chasin' a dream. I decided that although I'd been workin' the honky tonks for years, I hadn't really been puttin' the effort I should have into tryin' to get somewhere.

"I knew I didn't want to be fifty years old and playing in bars and honky tonks," he continued. "I felt what I wanted to do was be with a major label, making records. . . . I didn't feel like I was making any progress. . . . I thought maybe it was just something I dreamed up and it was never going to happen."

Despite the disappointments, Erv Woolsey and George Strait still weren't ready to give up. Erv managed to convince Chancey to come to Texas to see George and the Ace in the Hole Band in a San Marcos club. There, in a Texas bar, Chancey got to see what made George Strait so terrific. He heard the great-sounding Western swing that got couples dancing. He saw the undeniable charm of George Strait's looks and manners and how he attracted women without threatening men. It all looked good—but Chancey still didn't recommend that MCA sign him.

So Woolsey persuaded Chancey to come for a second time. For this occasion, Strait and the band played less Western swing. Chancey was still not fully convinced, but as he told *Billboard*, "He was doing more commercial-type stuff. . . . I went to talk to Jim [Fogelsong] and said he ought to give him a shot."

Although MCA Records had deemed the demo tape that Strait had recorded with Blake Mevis "too country," music publisher and producer Tom Collins also heard it, and was impressed. He offered to finance another demo session if Strait would include some of his company's songs. "So Blake and I go over there at night," Erv Woolsey recalled, "and listen, and we heard 'Unwound' and we both thought, 'Oh, man!' I said, 'Blake, this is the kind of song that I think can break him. This is his kind of stuff.' "

After hearing his demo of "Unwound," MCA Records finally decided to give George Strait that important first shot. He got a deal to record and release one single. If it was a hit, an album would follow.

And so, just a few months before the deadline he had set for himself to quit the business, Strait found himself signed, if only for one single, to the great Nashville label that boasted such stars as

Loretta Lynn, Conway Twitty, Merle Haggard, and Tanya Tucker. This had to be pretty exciting and just a little scary for a newcomer like George Strait. But it was exactly what he'd been hoping for.

He told *Billboard*, "They had everybody. I really did think that my record would get pushed under the pile." Strait wasn't wrong to worry. In any part of the entertainment business, the big stars bring in the big bucks for the companies and their work always gets top priority. "I remember when I first signed with MCA Records and I went into their offices in Nashville," Strait says. "I remember lookin' at all those gold records on the wall and thinking, 'Good grief, man!' "

Now it was time to see if maybe one day, a gold record by George Strait might hang on those walls, too.

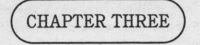

CHAPTER THREE

Welcome to Nashville

"The irony of 'urban cowboy' music was that when a good-looking real-life cattle roper and rancher named George Strait came along in 1981 with a pure Texas swing sound, no one took him seriously," said Jimmy Bowen. "He was almost like an outcast because he wasn't crossover material."

A native Texan himself, Jimmy Bowen had first come to Nashville around 1977, the year of Strait's first trip to Music City. A member of a popular group called the Rhythm Orchids who'd had a number-one hit single in 1957 called "I'm Stickin' with You," he soon gave up performing and became a producer. In the 1960s, he produced major radio hits and albums for Dean Martin, Frank Sinatra, and Sammy Davis, but in the early seventies he switched over to country, working with Mel Tillis and Hank Williams, Jr., among others. Bowen was to become a very important person in the life and career of George Strait.

In the early eighties, Nashville was full of people making country music who had never even sat on

54

a horse. They were wearing bell-bottoms and se-quined shirts and making pop music, using string sections, synthesizers, and the same drumbeats as everybody else.

George Strait came to Nashville ready to do whatever it took to move his career into a full-time gig and maybe even become known beyond the Texas border. He was prepared to cooper-ate with his producer, Blake Mevis, and MCA Records. He was ready to be guided by his good friend Erv Woolsey, who, more than anyone else, understood what George was about and what he was trying to achieve.

What he wasn't prepared to do was to take off his cowboy hat.

Strait didn't have any illusions about being able to do things his own way on his first record. Coming to Nashville to record a single for a ma-jor label—a single on whose success or failure everything was riding—was an opportunity he had dreamed of and worked toward. Given the deadline he had set for himself, if this didn't work, he'd be on the ranch for the rest of his life. Still, he wasn't going to deny his Texas heritage completely or the fact that at heart, he was and would always be a country singer.

In the booklet that accompanies *Strait Out of the Box*, his 1995 boxed set, he says, "When I came to town wearing a hat, that's all I ever heard: 'Take the hat off.' This is from people in the record business: 'Man, you sounded great, but take the hat off. Trust me, take the hat off.' But I never would do it. They were trying to make me into something else, but I was too hard-headed."

Tommy Foote, the former drummer of the Ace in the Hole Band and the group's road manager since 1982, said, "It wasn't any intentional attempt at image making; the hat is an extension of his personality. He always had a quiet determination about who he was and what he was going to do. He really is his own man."

"It's just that I identify with that sort of cowboy; those are the sort of people I run around with," Strait says. "I don't know, it's just a way of life."

On February 2, 1981—Groundhog Day—George Strait went into the studio to record "Unwound," written by Dean Dillon and Frank Dycus.

"We got through mixing it," Woolsey says. "I remember Blake and George walked across to my office, and I buzzed Ron. We went upstairs, played it for him, and he said, 'Yeah.' Sometimes it seems so easy."

Erv Woolsey's background as a radio promotion man convinced him that program directors in Texas and the Southwest would go for "Unwound." If the record got started in Texas, it could build from there.

The honky tonk dance beat and Texas fiddle at the heart of the song declared from the start that this record was different from what was coming over country radio at the time.

The lyrics of "Unwound" are also pure Texas honky tonk. "That woman that I had wrapped around my finger just come unwound." When asked if the story in the song was autobiographical, Strait replied, "No, it never really happened to me. But I think a lot of honky tonkers out there can really relate to that. I'm sure it's happened to a lot of people. It just really hasn't happened to me."

The single was released in May of 1981.

"Initially we had a little resistance from some stations who thought 'Unwound' sounded too traditional," Erv Woolsey said. "But once they started playing the record, we never heard from them again."

All artists remember the first time they heard their songs on the radio. George Strait was still working on the ranch at the time he heard "Unwound." "I was shocked," he recalls. "I couldn't believe it. I mean, hearing your first record on the radio, when it was something that you had been trying to get to do for so long, and then finally having it happen, it was wild. Here I was, driving around the ranch there, and I'd hear it go up the chart and I'm saying to myself, What's wrong with this picture? I've got a hit record. I need to go out and play some concerts!"

The week of May 16, 1981—the week of George Strait's twenty-ninth birthday—"Unwound" entered the *Billboard* country charts. Although *Billboard* is the music industry's most important publication, there are other charts that measure sales and radio play. *Billboard*'s, however, are the ones everyone hopes to make.

Then "Unwound" climbed into the top ten. It eventually went all the way to number six on the chart for the week of August 8. Not bad? How about downright miraculous for a debut single by an artist unknown in every state in the union except Hawaii and Texas!

The song stayed on the charts for most of the summer.

Suddenly the guy who had been too country was exactly country enough for the taste of American radio listeners. After the single exceeded everyone's expectations, MCA Records signed George Strait to a one-year contract. That's when he quit ranching to become a full-time country singer.

One person who heard "Unwound" on the radio was a nineteen-year-old student at Oklahoma State University in Stillwater. He was a kid who loved music, but whose tastes at that time ran to Kiss, the heavily made-up, hard-rock band. The young Oklahoman also admired the pop sounds of James Taylor and Dan Fogelberg.

"In the summer of my senior year," he recalled, "I was driving to the store with my dad, and this lady on the radio said, 'Here's a new kid from Texas and I think you're going to dig his sound.' " The lady played "Unwound" by then-new-kid George Strait.

"All of a sudden, it hit me. It was like, My God, I love this sound. That's it! That's what I'm gonna do!"

That Oklahoma State University student was Garth Brooks. "When I heard 'Unwound,' " he later said, "that's when I decided what I wanted to do."

Fan Fair takes place in Nashville every June. Thousands of people from all over America and the world pour into Music City to spend a week celebrating country music. Artists perform all over town, in hotels and clubs and concert halls. The fan clubs of the big stars set up booths, just as is done at trade shows or county fairs. Visitors stop by the booths and buy T-shirts and other merchandise, get photos of the stars, and learn about upcoming concert tours or new albums. For part of the week, the artists themselves come to the booths for a morning or afternoon.

That's when the real fun begins.

Fans will wait in line for hours and hours for the opportunity to spend a moment or two with the singers they love. The chance to get a handshake, an autographed picture, maybe a hug and a moment or two of conversation is at the heart of the fans' wish to come to Fan Fair.

In June of 1981, George Strait was one of the newest artists at Fan Fair, with a top-ten single that had the kind of country beat and lyrics that got under your skin. It was the perfect place for the new guy in town to make himself known to the country music world.

Each record company puts on a showcase of its

acts at Fan Fair. These live concerts are always packed with fans, industry people, and members of the media eager to see which acts the company is promoting for the upcoming summer concert season and fall record-buying time.

In 1981, MCA Records featured Brenda Lee, Barbara Mandrell, Loretta Lynn, and the Oak Ridge Boys. But the first act they wanted to show to the world was George Strait. It was a tremendous vote of confidence in their newest artist.

Every night of that Fan Fair week, George Strait and the Ace in the Hole Band played in the Reflections Ballroom at the Radisson Hotel in downtown Nashville. In a mirrored and chrome-plated room more suited to the disco music that had only recently been played there, fans were treated to something new and different: old-fashioned, traditional country music.

Reviewing the show in *Billboard* that July, Kip Kirby wrote, "Strait has a charisma that stretches out across the footlights, drawing an audience in to the music. Strait . . . represents the new breed of modern-day (forget urban) cowboy: authentic, intelligent, good-humored, handsome and skilled at more artistic ventures than roping cattle . . . one of the brightest new acts coming down the road in country music."

Country music fans throughout the world also had a chance to hear George Strait during Fan Fair week. He and the Ace in the Hole Band made a surprise appearance on the *Country Music Spec-*

tacular, the monthly live Radio Luxembourg broadcast that was heard by four million European, African, and Russian listeners.

While all this was going on, George was in the recording studio making his first album.

Although the Ace in the Hole Band had been his band for years, they didn't record the album with him. In Nashville, very few singers make their albums with their road bands. This is no reflection at all on the band or on the lead singer's relationship with it. It's a long-standing practice to record with session players, because studio musicians and live bands make two different kinds of music.

For one thing, the very qualities that make a live band great—raw energy, spontaneity, funky sound, and unpredictable jamming—don't translate in the studio. During a show, if a voice goes flat for a second or a couple of notes get dropped, it doesn't matter. What counts is the fun.

In the studio, however, it's a different story. When music is being recorded, and hopefully will be listened to again and again, there's little room for spontaneity. A record needs to be polished, organized, and carefully produced. Studio musicians have to play to exact specifications. These are players who have the ability to read music, listen to a demo once, and go in and play it perfectly the first or second time out. No doubt many of them can play live just as well as a road band, but in the studio, it is time for discipline, perfection, and the capacity to give an artist and producer exactly the kind of sound they're looking for.

Imagine how exciting it must have been for George Strait in June of 1981, playing music for Fan Fair every night and during the day recording his first album. Working around the clock was not new to him, but playing music during the daylight hours and getting paid for it sure was!

He realized what an amazing opportunity he'd finally gotten. "It's something that I've wanted the whole time," he said. "That's what everybody that's doing this kind of thing shoots for. So, I'm ready to do whatever it takes—go on the road, whatever it takes. It's just like any other business. You want to get to the top."

The producer of the album was Blake Mevis, who had produced "Unwound" and Darryl Staedtler's "Blame It on Mexico" during the earlier demo sessions. These songs became part of George Strait's debut album, which was released in September of 1981. It was called *Strait Country*.

Just before the album's release, Strait was asked how he felt about all those urban cowboys. "Well, they seem to like country music," he said. "I don't have anything against 'em. The only thing is, people see 'em and think they're what real cowboys are like, which isn't always so. For instance, not all real cowboys wear feathers all the way around their hats. But they like to go out and listen to country music, which is the main thing. We have that in common."

When asked if country music was coming back, he said, "Man, I really think it is. I think it might be going back to the hard-core country music."

He was also asked in 1981 if he'd ever ridden a mechanical bull. "Nah. I've ridden a real one . . . once," he said. "But once is enough for me. I tell you, it was exciting but it was also scary as hell. It was just a practice bull. . . . He took about two jumps and I was in the dirt."

Strait Country has some definite pop touches, perhaps more than the artist himself would have liked. But George Strait's mostly spare country songs and simple, clean-cut photograph on the cover left no doubt about his "country-ness" in a town and age of rhinestones, big hair, and slick country fashion.

Dallas Morning News reviewer Mike Rhyner would later say, "You gotta like the title of George Strait's debut album: *Strait Country*. Those two words tell you everything you need to know about the man, personally and musically."

The album's second single was "Down and Out," written by the "Unwound" writers, Dean Dillon and Frank Dycus. It reached the top twenty. The third single, written by Blake Mevis and David Wills, was "If You're Thinking You Want a Stranger (There's One Coming Home)." It was released in January of 1982 and peaked at number three in *Billboard* and number one in *Cash Box*.

"If You're Thinking You Want a Stranger" had

a new idea at its heart: that the man in the relationship might be responsible when things go wrong. Another album cut's title, "Every Time You Throw Dirt on Her (You Lose a Little Ground)," written by Michael Garvin and Tom Shapiro, also strikes this note of respect for women. These songs would be the first of several in which George Strait offered a little soul-searching for the guys.

On a spring night in New York City in 1982, George Strait and the Ace in the Hole Band were tuning up to play at the city's premier country music club. The Lone Star Café, located in Greenwich Village at Fifth Avenue and Thirteenth Street, several blocks north of Washington Square Park, was perhaps most famous for the huge sculpture of an iguana perched atop its roof. Some people called it the "Texas Embassy," alluding to the fact that Texas prides itself on being a nation as well as a state. Plenty of visitors to the Big Apple from the Lone Star State included the Lone Star Café on their list of places to visit.

The menu of Texas-style barbecue and great Texas beer kept the joint busy and the patrons well fed all evening. The music rarely started before midnight. And when it did, patrons were always certain to be tapping their feet to great concerts by the nation's top country music stars. Sometimes stars like Bob Dylan, who happened to have a home in the neighborhood, would show up unannounced to play.

The audience in the club that night was hot to hear the show by the new country singer causing so much talk on the city's country radio stations, WHN and WKHK. The long bar was packed three deep, and the tables were full. On the small stage to the right of the entry, the Ace in the Hole Band's equipment was set up. You could see its reflection in the mirror behind the stage that soared up for two stories. More folks were seated in the balcony at the top of a large winding staircase at the side of the stage.

Strait Country had been out for about six months. "Unwound" and "Down and Out" had been radio hits in New York, and favorites of the many country music fans who called the Big Apple home. "If You're Thinking You Want a Stranger" was climbing up the charts.

Given the situation, a lot of other new bands would simply have played every song from their album and tried their best to give the New York audience the kind of middle-of-the-road and even pop-country songs they figured those city folks wanted to hear.

Not George Strait. He and the Ace in the Hole Band played only four songs from *Strait Country*. Instead of going for the obvious and predictable, the guys from San Antonio played a dozen or so numbers from the deepest corners of traditional country. Of course, Bob Wills and George Jones were represented. Merle Haggard, too.

Jeff Nesin, a reviewer for the *Village Voice*, was in the audience that night, listening with the rest of the crowd to such gems as "Why Baby Why," "My Home in San Antone," "Milkcow Blues," and "Corrina Corrina." He wrote that these songs "were performed not as exotic museum pieces or burnished chestnuts, but as simple, relentless dance music that the new never wore off of."

Strait's "unadorned, straightforward (his name sure is apt) Texas neo-traditionalism has been one of the quiet pleasures of recent months," Nesin went on to write. Calling "Unwound" his favorite country radio song of the previous summer, he went on to praise "If You're Thinking You Want a Stranger" for featuring "Strait's no-nonsense, heart-in-his-throat voice at its most addictive."

The crowd at the Lone Star Café witnessed that up-close, small-club George Strait show that folks in Texas had enjoyed for years. Soon those clubs would be too small to hold the audiences who wanted to hear him.

And the next time George Strait played New York, it would be in Madison Square Garden.

Having three singles hit the charts in one year is more than a great start, it's phenomenal. This was especially true for a "traditional" country artist at a time of "crossover" and "pop-country" songs. So although it took George Strait years to achieve his first album, within months he was in the studio again recording his second.

Recording *Strait from the Heart* began in September 1981. It was also produced by Blake Mevis and had the same feel as the first: definitely country but still featuring some of those pop touches.

The songs on *Strait Country* and *Strait from the Heart* were selected by the album's producer and the record company. Being so new and still so grateful for the amazing opportunity he'd been given, Strait didn't object. He just sang them the way Mevis wanted him to.

It has to be intimidating for a new artist to find himself in a major Music City recording studio surrounded by professionals who've been making records for years. Such performers usually don't have the knowledge or experience to figure out what they can ask for and when they'd better keep their mouths shut. Under the circumstances, it's easy to understand Strait's accommodating attitude.

"Fool Hearted Memory," written by Byron Hill and Alan R. Mevis, was the first song recorded for the album. It is also the song that George Strait and the Ace in the Hole Band sang (actually lip-synched!) in a movie. (Called *The Soldier*, the film starred Ken Wahl; it concerned a group of Russian agents who steal enough plutonium to blow up the world.)

"We were in this scene in this club and a fight breaks out and we're supposed to keep on playing like nothing ever happened," Strait said. "That was pretty natural for us, since that did happen a lot back in the honky tonk days."

The cast and crew of the movie had so enjoyed working with George Strait and the Ace in the

Hole Band that they were in the audience when the band played at the Lone Star Café.

While recording *Strait from the Heart*, George was asked numerous times when he would be moving to Nashville. It was naturally assumed that he, like so many other artists who find success in the country music business, would be packing up the family and looking for a new home in Tennessee, and it's true that many aspiring singers, songwriters, and musicians who come to Nashville to make it do, in fact, stay. In addition to being the center of the country music business, it's a very friendly town whose citizens are some of the most generous, cordial, and hospitable people in the world. It's a great place to raise children, with fine schools, excellent recreational activities, and enough places of worship to keep all believers satisfied.

Being a musician in Music City is like living and working in a company town. Great musicians are everywhere, especially studio session players who can come in and cut songs on a moment's notice and make it sound like they've been playing them for years. Songwriters? Well, so many great songwriters call Nashville home that it's a local industry. People make appointments with each other to write and spend their nine-to-fives creating new songs just like any other career. There's live music of all kinds almost every night, and the air is charged with the energy of new artists looking to make their mark in music.

At the time, those asking George Strait when he was moving to Nashville must not have realized just how much of a Texan they were talking to. How could they know how deeply rooted he was in the Lone Star State? Or that the idea of leaving the ranching life he'd always known in the vast flatlands of south Texas did not appeal to him?

"I Can't See Texas from Here" was Strait's Western swing answer: he wrote it himself for *Strait from the Heart*. Nashville wasn't offended by the song—the lyrics acknowledged how much he liked Tennessee and how good all the folks there had been to him. George simply wasn't going to stay in a place where he couldn't see Texas.

In 1983, George moved into a new house in San Marcos with his wife, Norma, daughter, Jenifer, and son, Bubba. He meant it when he said he was going to stay in Texas!

Like all artists with albums to promote, George Strait hit the road after finishing *Strait from the Heart*. "Shoot," he said, "before the record we'd never played outside of Texas."

Some of the dates didn't pay enough to bring the Ace in the Hole Band, so George sang with pickup bands on the road. But when they could all go together, it was really exciting. "Making the transition from clubs to concerts was a major adjustment for me," he said. "In a club, if the people are up dancing, you know you're doing good. But to get the crowd reacting in a concert hall, that's another story."

How did he like those first big gigs outside of his home state?

"I kinda figured how it would be," he said. "But the crowd response in Texas and Oklahoma, I never expected that. Golly, it's amazing. Those people are standing there looking at me and it's neat. I really enjoy it. I'm not recognized much on the street, only if I have my hat on 'cause there's so many pictures of me in my hat, and I usually wear it when I sing.

"It feels great to be asked for an autograph. You know, when you work for this kind of recognition for so many years and finally start getting some, it feels really good."

"Fool Hearted Memory" was released as a single and went to number one, becoming George Strait's first chart topper. He and the band were playing at the Crystal Chandelier in Brownsville, Texas, when they got the news.

"It's just one of the best things that ever happened to me, to be involved in music," George Strait said in a 1981 interview with *Music City News*. "I just really enjoy it, I can't think of anything better to be into."

The song "Marina Del Rey," by Dean Dillon and Frank Dycus, is not country at all but very much a pop tune. When George Strait heard it, he liked it instantly. It is the story of a man remembering a long-ago love affair. Leading off the second side of *Strait from the Heart*, it must have been a little startling at first for those listeners expecting only country music from Strait's second album. It was an early indication that for George Strait, a good song was a good song no matter what category it was in. "Marina Del Rey" became a big hit for him and one that he frequently sings in concert to great applause all these years later.

Another ballad, "Amarillo by Morning," was written by Terry Stafford (who'd had a hit with it in 1974) and Paul Fraser. Strait and the Ace in the Hole Band had been performing it live for a long time. It tells the story of a professional rider who is tired of the rodeo and the effect it has on his life and relationships. He knows the only time it's worth it is those few seconds on the back of the bronco. Many people regard "Amarillo by Morning" as the first truly great song of Strait's career. It hit number four in the spring of 1983.

George Strait's second number-one single was the Darryl Staedtler song "A Fire I Can't Put Out." The lyrics spoke to everyone who had ever loved and lost, and that's just about all of us.

The success of the album was everything George Strait had dreamed of. He had believed for years that he could have a career in music, but it had taken a while to convince the rest of the world. Now the record company and the country music industry were beginning to see what all those fans in the Texas honky tonks and dance halls had known for a long time.

As Rick Mitchell of the *Houston Chronicle* wrote, "Strait's arrival on the national country scene in the early '80s was like a breath of fresh air. With Nashville pushing watered-down, pre-sweetened country pop formulas in a misguided crossover movement, sales had entered a slump that lasted until mid-decade. They called it 'country without the twang.' Country without the twang is like jazz without the swing, funk without the soul, rock without the roll. Who needs it?"

When pop-influenced country music started to decline and the powers that be in Nashville realized they needed something new to get record sales back up again, they turned to something old: good, traditional country music with real fiddles and steel guitars playing real music. The twang was back in.

The radio hits from *Strait Country* and *Strait from the Heart* led to great gigs on the road, and George Strait soon found himself with a golden spot on *the* big-ticket show that season: opening for Alabama, country's biggest act. He was also honored at radio appreciation days all over the South and Midwest. Meanwhile, *Billboard* selected him New Male LP Artist of the Year and *Record World* named him New Male Artist of the Year.

People were buying his records because they'd heard his singles on the radio and wanted to hear more. That's always been the purpose of singles: to stimulate sales of the albums. Country charts up to that time were based exclusively on radio play. One of the reasons for the rapidity of George Strait's rise was that in the early eighties, for the first time, actual radio airplay was being measured by computers.

It used to be that record companies' promotion people took advantage of their cozy relationships with radio programmers, not only to increase the times a certain record was played but to sometimes report a greater number of plays than was truthful. With computers recording the actual numbers of plays, and with an increase in the use of phone-in requests from listeners, the real voice of the people was being heard louder and clearer.

It would be almost a decade before sales charts were subjected to the same computerized overhaul. That's when the real sales power of country music would become undeniable.

"Unwound." "Down and Out." "If You're Thinking You Want a Stranger (There's One Coming Home)." Three hits—two of them top ten, one top five—from *Strait Country*. Then *Strait from the Heart* gave George Strait his first two number ones—"Fool Hearted Memory" and "A Fire I Can't Put Out." That second album also contained two more big hits, "Marina Del Rey" and "Amarillo by Morning," songs that to this day, even after twenty or so more albums, are considered among George Strait's best.

By the spring of 1983, George Strait, who had worried about getting lost in the pack of great country music artists on the MCA Records roster, had made himself one of the company's top acts.

The summer of 1983 found him and the Ace in the Hole Band touring the country in their bus, doing some of the things bands typically do on the road. "We watch a lot of movies and play a lot of poker. And I listen to a lot of tapes that are sent to me. Hopefully I'll find material for my albums," George told *The Tennessean* in July of '83.

There's a saying that you have your whole life to do your first piece of creative work, whether that work is a book, an album, a movie, a painting, or a sculpture. Then, if that's a success, you have a very short time to do more work or risk being forgotten by the very public that hadn't heard of you a year or two earlier anyway. And once you do that follow-up work, you're judged by even higher standards than before.

So, expectations for George Strait's third album were high. He was halfway through with its recording when he made it known that he didn't like the material producer Blake Mevis was bringing him to sing.

"The songs that we chose for the first album," he later said, "I didn't have just a hell of a lot to say about. Of course I would put my two cents' worth in, and I did think that the majority of the songs that we cut on there were good songs. But there're some songs that if I was to go back right now, I'd try to say, 'No, we're not gonna do that, not gonna do this.' But I didn't have that luxury then. I felt real lucky to be able to get in the studio and get a record deal here."

But now he'd had six hits from two albums. Strait told *Country Music* he and Blake Mevis "got to the point where we were buttin' heads right and left. . . . He really wanted me to go a little more towards pop-flavored tunes, and I just didn't want to do that, didn't feel comfortable with it at all. I'm the one who has to get up there every night and sing 'em and those just weren't the kind of songs I wanted to sing."

Another problem Strait had was Mevis's urging him to lose the cowboy hat. That wasn't going to happen. Nor was George Strait going to sing and record music he didn't believe in, music that wasn't country enough. Mevis pushed for more songs in the "Marina Del Rey" mold. Although George liked that song, he was still, in his heart and in his music, a dance-hall singer from Texas, and "Marina" didn't express that side of him.

"I wouldn't go for it," he told the *Houston Chronicle*. "I figured if ever there was a time to stand up for myself, this was it."

The upshot was that George Strait and Blake Mevis parted company and producer Ray Baker came on board. "Ray had cut Merle Haggard, and that was a big plus on Ray's side for me," Strait said. "And I listened to the stuff that he'd done, and I thought it sounded great. So that's who we decided on."

Right or Wrong, the only album George and Ray completed together, was released in October of 1983. The first single was "You Look So Good in Love" by Rory Bourke, Glen Ballard, and Kerry Chater. The song went to number one on the charts. A video was made for it, but Strait found it so corny and so embarrassing that he had the record company take it off the air. (See what a little clout can do?)

"You Look So Good in Love" was very pop sounding for someone who wanted to be really country, but the velvet sound of George Strait's voice on its lyrics makes his fans glad he recorded it. It's another example of a story in which a man sees his old love looking happy with someone new and accepts some responsibility for the failure of their relationship.

A tribute to one of George Strait's musical heroes, the last track they recorded turned out to become the title track of the album—an old Bob Wills tune called "Right or Wrong," written by Arthur L. Sizemore, Haven Gillespie, and Paul Biese. The Ace in the Hole Band had been playing it for years in the clubs, but putting it on the album was almost a last-minute decision. Johnny Gimble, a onetime Texas Playboy (and CMA's 1975 Instrumentalist of the Year), taught the other musicians the song and played fiddle on it. Gimble would go on to play a lot of fiddle with George Strait.

"Right or Wrong" became the album's second number-one hit. The third single, a waltz written by Dickey Lee, Tommy Rocco, and Johnny Russell, was "Let's Fall to Pieces Together." It, too, went to the top of the charts.

The album also included the first song Strait had recorded in his demos years earlier, Darryl Staedtler's "80 Proof Bottle of Tear Stopper." Another great tune was "Every Time It Rains (Lord Don't It Pour)," written by Keith Stegall and Charlie Craig.

What a whirlwind few years. Three albums, nine hits, and an amazing four consecutive number-one radio hits. Suddenly George Strait was seen as the future of country music . . . simply because he had followed his own instincts and gone back into its past.

Back in Texas, George Strait's earliest fans were surprised and glad. "The first time I heard him, I knew he had a good country voice, but there's just so many of them that sing there," said James White, owner of the Austin nightclub the Broken Spoke. "His drummer came up to me one night and told me, 'George is up there in Nashville doing some recording.' I kind of thought to myself, 'I've heard that story a lot of times,' and I knew they were real excited about it and I wished them luck—but sure enough, that's one of those stories where he went up there and was an overnight success."

There can be little doubt about how great George Strait must have felt in seeing his career take off with such incredible speed and success. He could play his music, continue to call Texas

his home, and support his family doing what he
loved. By early 1984, when it was time to start
working on a fourth album, the handsome singing cowboy from the Lone Star State had a lot
to be happy about. At the time, Jenifer was eleven
and Bubba (George Jr.) was four. All his family
and friends back in San Marcos, in San Antonio, and down in the ranch country near Pearsall
and Big Wells could proudly say they'd known
George Strait when.

Still, he wasn't thoroughly satisfied with the
way his music was going. Many artists would be
content to be well-known radio hit makers and
chart-topping album sellers. While grateful and
humble for what he had achieved, Strait wanted
something else. He wanted more control over his
own artistic career. He wanted the music to
sound the way he heard it in his heart and mind.
He definitely wanted to keep it country.

He and Ray Baker had nearly completed ten
new tracks, and plans were in place to release the
new album in the fall when, in April of 1984,
Strait was chosen as the Academy of Country
Music's Male Vocalist of the Year.

Based in Los Angeles, the Academy of Country
Music is the younger sibling to the CMA. Established in 1964 to enhance and promote the
growth of country music, it sponsors industry
seminars, performance showcases for artists, and
many charity benefits. While the CMA Awards
are a fall ritual, the ACMs happen every spring.

To be chosen as the ACM's Male Vocalist of the

Year was George's first big award and a true endorsement of the work he had done over the past
three years. But that award, coupled with the
previous hits, upped the stakes for his future.
What would happen if he released a less-than-
great album receiving not-so-generous reviews
and producing fewer hit singles than its predecessors? How long a roll, after all, could one artist be on?

In May, Jim Fogelsong left MCA Records and
was replaced by Jimmy Bowen as the head of
the country music division. Bowen had been in
Nashville for about seven years and had made his
mark as a brilliant producer of country music
and a record-company executive who "fixed"
record companies. Bowen was tough: he would
come into companies, make huge changes in personnel and direction, and get great results, selling lots of records.

According to his autobiography, *Rough Mix*,
written with Jim Jerome, three months before
Bowen took over MCA Records, he called Erv
Woolsey and set up a meeting. Bowen knew how
hard Woolsey had worked to sign George Strait
to MCA when the label head Jim Foglesong and
A&R head Ron Chancey were less than enthused.
"Knowing my reputation for taking over and
cleaning house, Erv pretty much knew what was
coming down," Bowen writes. "I told him he
should go pack his things and leave MCA."

Erv was one step ahead of Bowen. He was

ready to take the opportunity his departure from MCA offered him to set up his own personal management company and have George Strait as his main client.

When he heard the news, Jimmy Bowen told Erv, "Well, then, I guess we need to have a real good working relationship."

"Contrary to what a lot of people think, Jimmy Bowen was a huge help. . . . Jimmy did a lot of great things for me," Erv Woolsey says, "and helped me get my company started and those are the kind of things I'll always be grateful to him for."

What George Strait would always be grateful to Jimmy Bowen for was that Bowen gave him the only piece of the success puzzle he'd been missing: control over his music.

Bowen had a reputation as an artist's producer. He felt his main job was to help artists make exactly the records they wanted.

George told him, "I've got ten tracks done and I'm never going to put my voice on 'em—and I'm never workin' with Ray again. . . . They're not my tracks," he said. "I didn't participate in any of 'em. They give me the song to learn and then I had to sit on the couch in the studio and have a beer while the producer and the band got the track ready. Then they said, 'Ready, George,' and I went out and sang the lyrics."

Bowen suggested that George scrap the ten songs, fire Ray Baker, and begin coproducing his own albums. That gave George the green light he'd been waiting for.

Much as he'd liked working with Ray Baker, he thought his input in the process hadn't been taken as seriously as he would have liked. "The reason Ray and I kind of parted ways is . . . he had a certain way that he wanted to do things in the studio," Strait says. "And back then I felt intimidated anyway. Just goin' in the studio. I was so green, and . . . I was real nervous about [it]. We had great pickers in there that worked with all these great artists. . . . And then when I did feel like I had something to say in there, it just didn't feel like it mattered."

George had been uneasy with everyone telling him what to play. "It might have just been because of my nervousness in the studio, but when I was working with those other producers, I was a little bit afraid to put my own two cents' worth in. . . . But I know I shouldn't have felt like that, because it's my music that's going out there."

Jimmy Bowen told George that the music, the records, and the sound were his and that George should make the decisions. "You've got the look, the sound, the voice, but it's gonna be your own. Not mine.

"We'll sell platinum," Bowen told him. "I'll put together a band doing George Strait music that'll knock your hat in the dirt, pal. Trust me."

George said, "That is what I want to do."

As he had done with other artists he produced, Jimmy Bowen went to see George Strait live and also got a tape of his show. He felt it was important to capture on record George's distinctive Texas swing sound. "Bowen thought something was missing in my records," George says. "He came out and saw one of our shows and felt like my originality in concerts didn't come across on record."

Coproducing an album with Jimmy Bowen gave Strait two remarkable opportunities. One was the input of a legendary producer who had worked to create some of the best music of some of Strait's most beloved heroes, from Frank Sinatra to Merle Haggard and Hank Williams, Jr.

The other was the chance to do most of the work himself. "Jimmy Bowen offered me the opportunity to take more control over what I was doing in the studio by letting me coproduce my own albums. . . . And he just said it flat out to me—he said, 'These are your records, not mine. You need to be making the decisions.' And he says, 'Your sound, not mine. If I make the record I'm gonna make my record, you're just gonna be singing it.' Which makes a lot of sense for everybody. So he allowed me to do that, and I've been doing it ever since."

Being your own producer means being completely responsible for everything on the album, from choosing the songs to supervising the arrangements, from directing the way the musicians play the songs to the way the engineers mix them. Selecting the singles that will promote the album to the radio-listening audience is a crucial production decision.

"This time I really listened to a lot of songs and picked the material myself. I went around to all the major publishers and listened hard," George recalls. "Before, I had always been handed a list of songs my producer had picked out and I had to choose from those. Jimmy let me do pretty much what I wanted to do in the studio."

Strait found songs by some of Music City's best old-school honky tonk songwriters. Mack Vickery and Wayne Kemp, who had cowritten Johnny Paycheck's "I'm the Only Hell (Mama Ever Raised)," gave George "The Fireman." Sonny Throckmorton, best known for "The Last Cheater's Waltz," gave him "The Cowboy Rides Away," cowritten with Casey Kelly.

THEY WRITE THE SONGS

It would take a whole other book to tell the stories of the amazing songwriters who have given George Strait his long string of hits. Here are just a few of the giants whose words and music bring so much pleasure to George Strait and his fans.

HANK COCHRAN

"The Chair," "Ocean Front Property"
For five decades, the songs of Hank Cochran have entertained millions. "Little Bitty Tear" and "Funny Way of Laughing" were big hits for Burl Ives. Patsy Cline had a huge success with "I Fall to Pieces," which Cochran wrote with Harlan Howard. Born in Isola, Mississippi, Cochran roamed Texas, New Mexico, and California, where he was part of a rock group called the Cochran Brothers. As a songwriter and song plugger in Nashville, he was the first to publish the songs of Willie Nelson.

DEAN DILLON

"Unwound," "Marina Del Rey," "The Chair,"
"Ocean Front Property," "If I Know Me,"
"Easy Come, Easy Go," "Nobody in His
Right Mind Would've Left Her,"
"Lead On," and many more
Born in the Tennessee coal belt north of Knoxville, Dillon began writing when he was given a guitar at the age of nine. At fourteen, he was performing on a Knoxville TV program. He came to Nashville in 1973 and worked odd jobs, including performing at Opryland USA, until he became a full-time songwriter. "I was born to be and have always been a songwriter," he says. George Strait says, "If Dean's not the best writer in town, he's one of the top two."

HARLAN HOWARD

"I've Seen That Look on Me (a Thousand Times)," "Someone Had to Teach You," "Anything You Can Spare," "Her Only Bad Habit Is Me," and "I've Got a Funny Feeling"

The dean of Nashville songwriters, Harlan Howard has also been called the Irving Berlin of country music. In a career spanning six decades he has written or cowritten about four thousand songs, including "Heartaches by the Number" and "I Fall to Pieces." His songs have been made famous by artists of all kinds, from Ray Charles to the Judds, from Conway Twitty to k. d. lang. Born and raised on a farm in Michigan, Howard worked in a factory in Los Angeles and wrote songs before moving to Nashville. In 1961, he had fifteen songs in the Top 40 country charts, a feat never equaled by any other songwriter.

SANGER D. "WHITEY" SHAFER

"Does Fort Worth Ever Cross Your Mind?" "Lefty's Gone," "All My Ex's Live in Texas," and many more

In 1967, an aspiring singer moved from Whitney, Texas, to Nashville with three songs he had written. Whitey Shafer got a writing deal with Ray Baker's Blue Crest Music, and two of the three songs were cut by George Jones. He did get his chance to record but never charted a record. The first song he wrote with his drinking buddy Lefty Frizzell, "That's the Way Love Goes," won a Grammy for Merle Haggard. He has gone on to be one of country music's top songwriters.

"When I got the opportunity to coproduce that album, I made myself really do a lot more work than I had ever even thought about doing for a record," Strait says. "I would go song by song. . . . I involved myself so much in that record, as far as the arrangements of the tunes, and what instrumental part was gonna be here and what was gonna be there."

Just as he'd promised, Jimmy Bowen gathered a band of great studio musicians: Reggie Young and Larry Byron on electric guitar. Eddie Bayers on drums. Randy Scruggs on acoustic guitar. John Hobbs on piano. Hank DeVito on steel. David Hungate on bass. Curtis Young on harmony vocals. George suggested Johnny Gimble for fiddle, after his successful playing on "Right or Wrong."

If, during work on the album, some of the musicians happened to ask Bowen questions about the arrangement, he would tell them it wasn't his record and to ask George. At that moment the laid-back and relaxed George Strait realized it really *was* his record. "You could feel the energy kick up on both sides of the glass," Bowen says. "The players loved cutting those tracks."

George Strait was in charge and working to the best of his ability. The musicians were excited to be involved in something they instinctively knew was very special. The ten songs on the album were cut in three days. Perhaps a little fast, but the energy was there to make it happen, and the fans had already been waiting too long.

When Bowen had come to Nashville in the late 1970s, he'd been amazed at the outdated, old-fashioned, low-tech studios cranking out the music. He made it his mission to update the technology, bringing it up to the sophisticated level of studios in New York and Los Angeles. This meant changing from analog to digital, among other things. Bowen convinced the majority stockholder of Nashville's Sound Stage Studio to invest in updating his facilities. In return, he promised to lease it for a year and use it five days a week.

Does Fort Worth Ever Cross Your Mind, the first *real* George Strait album in terms of his own artistic vision, was recorded in that studio. Not a bad place for George Strait to produce his first album. As Bowen writes, that studio helped "top acts like Strait, Reba, and the Oak Ridge Boys make music that sounded every bit as full and clear as Elton or the Eagles."

During the summer of 1984, George and the Ace in the Hole Band were on the road again.

They called the summer tour the "George Strait Texas Dance Hall Tour," and took their trademark honky tonk and Western swing to some big arenas to meet the increasing demand for tickets to a George Strait show. In some places, they brought a dance floor into the arenas so fans could dance during the concerts.

When the dance floor couldn't be used anymore, Strait remarked, "It's a shame. Sure is a waste of good dance music."

Does Fort Worth Ever Cross Your Mind was released in September 1984. The title track was the album's first single and went to number one, making it George Strait's fifth consecutive number-one single. The moment he heard the song he'd fallen in love with the great story, the wonderful melody, and, no doubt, the fact that it mentions not one but two of Texas's most majestic cities.

Cowritten by Sanger D. Shafer, known familiarly as Whitey, who is famous for his work and friendship with the legendary Lefty Frizzell, and Darlene Shafer, "Does Fort Worth Ever Cross Your Mind" is as heart-wrenching a song as Strait has ever recorded. In a story of love and the pain of heartbreak that won't go away, the singer wonders if his former love even remembers their time together. The possibility that she doesn't is even more awful than the pain of their breakup.

In "You're Dancin' This Dance All Wrong," written by John Porter McMeans and Ron Moore, the singer is having a hard time getting in step with a new partner. Soon, though, their rhythms fit together just fine. Strait's voice on this song is amazingly rich and clear.

In November 1984, *Right or Wrong* became George Strait's first gold record, selling more than half a million copies. *Does Fort Worth* was certified gold in April of 1985, six months after it came out, before the second single was released. That song was "The Cowboy Rides Away," which Strait still uses to close many of his concerts.

Another favorite hit was the third single, "The Fireman." The *Houston Chronicle* raved, "A hot-tempoed and cleverly written lyric about a ladies' man whose mission in life is patrolling town 'puttin out old flames,' it is apt to start a forest fire among Strait's smoldering legions of female fans."

All the fans loved it. "Ever since we released the album," Strait said at the time, "we've gotten a lot of response to that song. I have people all the time giving me coffee cups, T-shirts, and everything else with 'fireman' written on them— even flags from fire departments."

Songs set in the Lone Star State or with the names of Texas cities in the titles were already becoming a feature of George Strait albums. "It's pure coincidence," Strait said at the time about "Does Fort Worth Ever Cross Your Mind" and "Amarillo by Morning." "They were strong songs. 'Amarillo by Morning' was one we'd been doing for a long time before I recorded it. That's why we released it."

Does Fort Worth Ever Cross Your Mind is a loosely connected collection of songs about a man struggling with love lost, love rediscovered, and maybe some new love for the future. As his first effort as producer, it demonstrated that Strait had an amazing ear for a great song, a gift he would use again and again in his brilliant career. His love for simple yet rich arrangements showcased the talents of each musician on the record.

Some people have commented that the record sounds live. Bowen liked to bring all the musicians in at once and have them record together rather than laying tracks one at a time. A lot of albums are put together like puzzles, with the parts being recorded at different times, sometimes on different days. It's hard to generate much excitement with this assembly-line approach. But with everyone there, playing together, an energy sometimes comes through for the listener that resembles the effect of a live performance.

Something else makes this a great album as well. When he was finally in charge of his own music, George Strait could stop worrying about singing and sounding like what someone else wanted him to be. Instead, here he is confident enough to be himself.

Does Fort Worth Ever Cross Your Mind is hard country, entirely traditional, drawing deeply from the roots that were planted by such giants as Merle Haggard and Lefty Frizzell. It is considered classic George Strait and one of the greatest albums of his distinguished career.

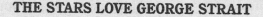

THE STARS LOVE GEORGE STRAIT

"I have known George Strait for many years and it has been my pleasure to see his career go straight—no pun intended—up to the rank of superstar. He is a hard-working and caring person, a great country music singer, good actor, great guy, and fellow Texan."

—George Jones

"I've been a big George Strait fan ever since I heard 'Unwound' on the radio in Charlotte, North Carolina. I also sang a lot of his music in the clubs through the seventies and early eighties."

—Randy Travis

"I like what he has done with his music and his career. I'm proud to know him and he is one of my favorite singers."

—Merle Haggard

"I am doing what I am doing today because of the Good Lord, my family, and George Strait."

—Garth Brooks

"One person whose career I've always admired, and his music, too, is George Strait. . . . He just keeps coming out with great music."

—Alan Jackson

"George will always go down in my book as one of the great vocalists and great entertainers in our business."

—John Anderson

"His voice is just so rich and powerful, yet beautiful. When he sings a song, that sucker's going to number one. We've got all of his albums at our house, and we love listening to them."

—Billy Ray Cyrus

"He's my biggest idol. . . . George is a nice, nice man, and I've gotten to sing with him a couple times. I love his music, always have."

—John Michael Montgomery

"I've competed with a lot of different people, but I have my special people that I love to compete with. George and I have always competed. I love him, but I love to compete, too."

—Reba McEntire

"I buy all his albums, everything he puts out. That's the kind of career I want—like George Strait."

—Tracy Byrd

"George Strait's body of work will stand the test of time as well as a Hank Williams, George Jones, or anybody else. I admire George Strait a lot for his consistency and the earthiness he brings to the table."

—Marty Stuart

CHAPTER FOUR

Nice Guys Finish First

George Strait was on the tiny island of Bimini in April of 1985 when *Does Fort Worth Ever Cross Your Mind* won the Album of the Year award from the Academy of Country Music.

This was one month after the release of *George Strait: Greatest Hits*, compiling the hits that had come from *Strait Country*, *Strait from the Heart*, and *Right or Wrong*.

The Academy of Country Music also named him Top Male Vocalist of the Year for the second year in a row.

"I almost hate to say it, but I was bonefishing in the Bahamas," Strait told the *Houston Chronicle*. "We were doing a fishing show, *The Country Sportsman*, with Bobby Lord." The show aired on The Nashville Network.

The staff and guests at the hotel saw the show on TV and came over to tell Strait, who was having dinner with his buddies, that he had won. "We were all pretty tired that night and were fixing to just finish eating and go to bed, but we

kind of had to go out and celebrate after that,"
he said.

Strait wished he'd gone to the awards ceremony in Hollywood, but when the plans were being made for the fishing show, he didn't think he
would win.

The first George Strait album over which he
had a large measure of creative control was a
huge success, both artistically and commercially.
This brought his career up yet another level. His
concert crowds were growing bigger all the time.
To meet the demand Strait kept adding more and
more dates in the summer of 1985.

"I could see a change," he says. "I mean, I was
working my tail off back then. I was doing just, I
don't know, two hundred dates. I was just on the
road, constantly on the road. But you could see a
change in the crowds, you could see a change in
the reaction of people to you when you did shows."

One change was the reaction of women. They
couldn't get enough of George Strait's handsome
face, piercing green eyes, and warm Texas grin.
At all the George Strait and the Ace in the Hole
Band concerts, women of all ages were handing
flowers up to him onstage. Some were actually
flinging their underwear at him. Fans of both
sexes were tossing their boots onto the stage to be
autographed.

One woman was seen at a concert in Texas crying her eyes out because she believed George
Strait had waved at *her*.

If you've been to a George Strait concert, you know that he sure doesn't make a spectacle of himself onstage like some artists do. He doesn't leap and jump all over the place. There's no smoke and fancy lights. What George Strait does is stand there in his pressed jeans, button-down shirt, cowboy hat, and cowboy boots, holding and playing his guitar and singing right into the microphone. He looks out to the audience, smiling and twinkling his eyes. It's obvious he's having a genuinely good time.

"I'm not a comedian," he says. "I can't even tell a good joke. The people come out to hear me sing, so that's what I go out and do."

Ben Farrell, promoter of Strait's Houston Summit concerts, says, "The thing is, there's nothing calculated about it. There's not a fictitious bone in his body. He appeals to women, but he's a man's man. He's a military veteran, a college graduate, and rodeo cowboy. Plus he's an awful good singer. He's very much a class act."

The *Houston Chronicle* called Strait "the hottest thing to come out of the southwest since the all-day bareback ride. As cleanly and bashfully handsome as cinematic cowboys of filmdom's golden age."

Each month the concert schedule got busier. George Strait told *People* magazine, "I'd be crazy to slow down right now; things are going too good. I have to hit it full steam until I can't stand it anymore."

In June of 1985, he started to move his shows

to bigger venues. He was preparing for his first stints in Las Vegas and the Universal Amphitheater in Los Angeles, in tandem with Merle Haggard and Alabama.

The big concert promoters were discovering what had been happening for years in the smaller shows in the Southwest. There, nightclub owners had been known to pile bales of hay in front of stages to protect Strait from overzealous females.

How did country music's newest rising star feel about all this? Did he mind all the attention?

"Shoot, no. In fact, I prefer it," he has said. "I like that a lot better than when you've got a sit-down audience in an auditorium where it's like you're watching a movie or something."

The beginning of the return to country music's past coincided with the two terms of President Ronald Reagan. Reagan offered a vision of a new yet old-fashioned America: prosperous, secure, and steeped in the traditional values our country was founded on. It was just the kind of country that would love good old country music.

The music business and the entertainment press were starting to pay attention to a new group of musicians that had been dubbed "New Traditionalists." Randy Travis, a singer from North Carolina with a great voice, had a major-selling debut album called *Storms of Life*. His hit single "On the Other Hand" had people saying he was the new generation's answer to George Jones.

A fiery redhead from Oklahoma, Reba McEntire, was another artist on MCA Records. Her career had blossomed after Jimmy Bowen told her the same thing he'd told George Strait: make your own music your own way. Ricky Skaggs had produced his own first album and had two number-one singles right off the bat.

THE NEW TRADITIONALISTS

In the pop-influenced 1970s, these artists were considered "too country." By the mid-eighties, they, along with George Strait, were dubbed the "New Traditionalists" and credited with moving country music forward . . . by returning it to its traditional sounds.

THE JUDDS

The mother-and-daughter duo's acoustic bluegrass music got them through some early hard times. But their first album yielded two number-one singles in 1984—"Mama He's Crazy" and "Why Not Me?" A Grammy, an ACM award, and the CMA's Horizon Award soon followed. Continuing an unbroken string of hits through the eighties and nineties, Naomi and Wynonna Judd have brought the music of the Kentucky hills to millions.

REBA McENTIRE

A freckle-faced redhead from Oklahoma with a dynamite set of pipes, Reba got her start singing for—and riding in—the rodeos. Like George Strait, she was first dismissed as too country, but soon that's just what audiences loved about her, buying her albums by the millions. Spectacular concerts, dramatic videos, movie roles, numerous awards, and a best-selling autobiography maintain her status as a megastar with a magnificent voice.

RICKY SKAGGS

He played the mandolin at the age of five and mastered the guitar at eight. He joined Emmylou Harris's Hot Band and recorded with her before launching his own successful solo career. Ricky's self-produced first major album had two number-one hits in 1982, earning him a slew of major awards. The hits have kept on coming for the last fifteen years, ranking Skaggs as the first of the New Traditionalists and one who's still at the top.

RANDY TRAVIS

His *Storms of Life* made country music history by becoming the first debut album of a solo country artist to sell more than a million copies in less than a year. The North Carolina native, with a plaintive, twangy voice that sounds like the young Merle Haggard, arrived on the scene in 1985. Also dismissed as "too country," Travis had nine number-one hits from 1986 to 1989. Today, he is considered one of country's top stars.

These so-called New Traditionalists of the early 1980s sang songs that weren't quite as old-fashioned about love as those of George Jones or as hard-hitting about real-life issues as the music of Merle Haggard. But they were playing the kind of old country music arrangements many listeners were searching for. Folk and bluegrass met blues and jazz, honky tonk and rockabilly combined with Western swing, all reflecting that Reagan-era nostalgia for the past.

George Strait had been making music that could classify him as a New Traditionalist since 1981. He was right at the heart of a trend he'd probably never even thought of starting.

Something Special, another Strait and Bowen coproduction, was released in August 1985. The album had even more Texas swing music than usual, and reminded everyone where George Strait really came from.

The number-one hit "The Chair," written by Dean Dillon and Hank Cochran, is the kind of song that makes you understand when people say great songs do as much with a story in three minutes as some books do in three hundred pages. In this case, it's the story of a man in a bar who shyly and tentatively approaches a woman by telling her that she's taken his chair. As the song progresses they share a drink and a dance and make a connection with each other. Then he admits at the end that the chair wasn't his after all.

Another single, "You're Something Special to Me," written by David Anthony, is a beautiful ballad that Strait sings in the style of Tommy Duncan, a lead singer with Bob Wills and the Texas Playboys. It made it to number four. The song is notable for its blending of pop with honky tonk.

Something Special also contained the sad song "Haven't You Heard?" by Wayne Kemp. It's the story of a man who has convinced his lover to leave her husband, who also happens to be his friend. Even worse, the couple's child is torn apart, saying, "Haven't you heard, Daddy's gone crazy?" Another song, "Lefty's Gone," by Whitey Shafer, is a tribute to the great Texas singer Lefty Frizzell. Shafer writes, "It's not right that Lefty's gone."

Record executives, radio programmers, fans, and especially other artists admire George Strait for his amazing ability to pick hit material. He described the process in an interview with *Country Beat* magazine as "pretty simple, actually. All the publishers keep up with who's going in the studio when, and as soon as they find out you've got a date booked, they start sending you all kinds of material. You get tapes and tapes and more tapes and you just listen and listen and listen and try to find the best ones you can. I go through hundreds of tapes."

Every big artist has his or her pick of the best material being written in Nashville and elsewhere in the country. Some songwriters create music just for the enjoyment of the art, but most really want their songs to be recorded. When an artist as big as George Strait makes an album, it's many songwriters' dream to have a cut on it.

What does Strait look for in a song? "I think it's the melody, mostly. The melody is what catches my ear and I think it catches a lot of people's ears, and they just don't know it. And then you start listening to the lyrics. That's the way that I've found that I do it anyway. If the melody sounds really good, well, then I start listening to the lyrics and see what they say."

Strait says he and his producers never argue about a song. "If I don't like it, I'm not going to cut it. That's just the way it is. I'm not going to do it. So that makes it easy.

"Ultimately you're the one who lives and dies by the song. You're the one who has to go out there and sing it every night."

Something Special was released in September 1985, one month before the Country Music Association Awards.

Just as the Academy of Country Music had honored *Does Fort Worth Ever Cross Your Mind* as

Album of the Year, so did the Country Music Association.

George Strait was also named Male Vocalist of the Year.

Back in San Marcos, Texas, the Cheatham Street Warehouse was having an anniversary party. Kent Finlay, then owner of the club, says he used to tell people, back in the seventies, that George Strait was going to be a star.

"What's he doing playing here?" they would say.

After he'd made it big, George Strait brought the Ace in the Hole Band back to the Cheatham Street Warehouse to play for the hometown fans.

"What happened is, it wasn't safe for him," said Finlay. "The place only holds about three hundred people; how do you keep all those others out? It wasn't a wise thing to do. But the last time George played for me, he wouldn't take any money. He is, really and truly, one of the nicest guys you'll ever meet."

Finlay got the last laugh. At the anniversary party around the time of the CMA Awards, he put up a big sign that said I TOLD YOU SO.

George was so flustered by winning his first CMA Award that he forgot to thank Jimmy Bowen. "He never really said much about it," Strait says, "but I could tell that I'd really screwed up."

Other New Traditionalists besides Strait won CMA Awards in 1985. The Female Vocalist of the Year was Reba McEntire. Ricky Skaggs took the

Entertainer of the Year award and his band won for Instrumental Group of the Year. Vocal Group of the Year went to the talented mother-and-daughter team, the Judds, and their song "Why Not Me?" took Single of the Year.

George Strait was asked about the apparent conflict between traditional and new/pop country. "Everybody has to ask me about that," he said, "but I really hate to get into it. Yeah, there's more traditional-type country around than there was seven or eight years ago, and I hope that continues. I'm a country singer, but when I'm looking for songs to do, I don't go out with a specific kind of song in mind. I just look for a *good* song.

"Whether it's traditional or contemporary doesn't matter to me; if I hear it and I like it, I can do it the way I want to do it. I mean, 'Marina Del Rey' and 'The Chair'—to me, those aren't traditional hard-core country-sounding records; but I feel like they're good songs, and they were good for me. That's why I did them."

The *George Strait: Greatest Hits* album went gold in November of 1985. The holiday season was a time of great satisfaction for George Strait and his family. Just five or six years earlier, he had almost given up on being a country singer. Now he was one of the biggest, if not the biggest, country singer in America. More than that, he had achieved his stardom singing the songs he wanted to sing, arranging them and having them played the way he heard them in his heart.

He'd also kept his hat on. Now nobody was telling him to take it off.

All of his success had everyone talking about new and different opportunities for him. Offers for all kinds of new ventures always pour in to the management offices and record companies of big stars. It takes a lot of clear thinking and common sense not to let stardom go to your head and take you in directions you may not want to go in.

In early 1986, George Strait said, "I feel real blessed to be where I am. I'm not about to give it up. There's been talk about movies and TV and stuff, but I'm pretty much involved in the country music business. My record company has its own ideas about this, but my opinion is that when actors and singers try to trade roles, ninety percent of the time it doesn't work. There are exceptions, of course, but not many.

"So I'm happy singing country music, and I would be happy if I never did a picture in my whole life. There's nothing wrong with branching out, but you can't let go of the thing that made you. I'm gonna be a country singer till I die."

Stars in all fields get endorsement and sponsorship deals that bring them good money and sometimes the chance to tour the country on someone else's dime. George Strait was no stranger to this, but one of the deals just may have been a little nearer to his heart.

In 1986, Strait signed a licensing agreement

with Resistol hats to make a George Strait line. Irving Joel, president of Resistol, issued an announcement saying the company had made special hats for the star for a long time. "It was only natural that we should become his licensee," Joel said. "We feel confident that a product bearing his name will be extremely popular in the marketplace." Hats were offered in two price groups: one for the first-time wearer and one for the aficionado of Western apparel.

In May 1986, George Strait's seventh album—appropriately titled #7—was released to even greater acclaim than his others. #7 had the same winning mix of honky tonk, Western swing, and country and western standards fans of all ages were coming to expect.

The single "Nobody in His Right Mind Would've Left Her," written by Dean Dillon, was a number-one hit. It was one of the songs Strait had demoed years earlier. The second single was "It Ain't Cool to Be Crazy About You," written by Royce Porter and Dean Dillon. It also went to number one. The album included "Cow Town," written by Hal Burns and Tex Ritter, "Deep Water," written by Fred Rose, which had been recorded by Bob Wills and the Texas Playboys, and "Rhythm of the Road," written by Dan McCoy, a rock-and-roll style song about the rigors of nonstop touring. That was a subject George Strait was an expert on, since by this time he and the Ace in the Hole

Band were doing some two hundred and fifty shows a year.

On the stage, a George Strait show wasn't anything like a rock concert. The artist stood at the mike, singing and playing his guitar while the Ace in the Hole Band made their always excellent music behind him. But to see the audiences you'd have thought they were watching Led Zeppelin or Bruce Springsteen. The reaction of the crowds, from young kids to their grandparents, was wild.

Bob Claypool of *The Houston Post* wrote, "Strait may look like a matinee idol, but his music is pure and unadulterated and real. And it's the tough stuff, too; country music from fifty years' worth of dance hall nights and Saturday night brain-fries. All of this is infused with Strait's no-frills, warm and sincere vocals, and the hot licks of the Ace band."

"George loves to have the fans up close, as close as they can get to the stage to where they can walk up and take pictures," Erv Woolsey told reporters. "He loves to look out there and see 'em being happy. He sees them having fun and he plays off that. It makes it more fun for him."

THE CRITICS HAVE THEIR SAY

"It's too easy to suggest that George Strait has profited tremendously from his clean-cut good looks and Sensitive Hunk image ... he really hasn't cut a bad record ... and therein lies the secret of his success."

—David McGee,
Rolling Stone Album Guide

"It takes time for even the most gifted musicians to mature, and everything about George Strait's performance—from his skilled vocals to the tasteful, elaborate production values—was a tangible notch above."

—Randy Lewis, *Los Angeles Times*

"Sometimes you wonder: Is country music getting worse or is Strait just getting better and better?"

—David Zimmerman, *USA Today*

"In sixteen years, George Strait has scarcely cut a song without some redeeming quality, much less released a whole album of them, which is why his career has come to resemble Nashville's answer to the Energizer Bunny: He just keeps on going while others fall by the wayside."

—Rick Mitchell, *Houston Chronicle*

"George Strait isn't a phony, and that isn't faint praise. . . . Those who still look to country for the simple things treasure

Shooting Star/Ron Davis

Globe/Lisa Rose

More awards than he can count—Academy of Country Music
(left) and the Country Music Association (right)

Rick Henson Photography

The Ace in the Hole Band

Mark Tucker

Rick Hunter

Rick Henson Photography

Like Elvis, George sold out his first appearance
at the Las Vegas Hilton

George with Willie Nelson

George outside the Lone Star Café during his first New York
City appearance in 1982

George Strait carries on Bob Wills's tradition of Western swing

Mr. and Mrs. John Strait with Mr. and Mrs. George Strait

Norma and George   Jenifer and George Jr. (Bubba)
in the early 1980s with their dad

If he weren't a country music star, George would be a rodeo rider . . .

. . . but then his adoring fans would miss his great music

the matter-of-fact commitment of the man, who could have been named by a press agent, but wasn't."
—Robert Cristgau,
Christgau's Record Guide: The 80s

"George Strait continues to get better and better. Partly, it's the maturity in his voice and the authority that it carries. It's also the songs. It's unlikely that there's anyone in country with a better ear for songs."
—Chet Flippo, *Billboard*

"George Strait's voice . . . is as familiar and welcomed as a comfortable pair of Wranglers and broken-in Justin boots."
—Mario Tarradell,
Country: The Essential Album Guide

In a review of #7 in *Rolling Stone* magazine, hardly a publication one would associate with country music, James Hunter said that it was time to stop thinking of George Strait as "the white Stetsoned sheriff of country's current 'new traditionalism.' Think of him instead as Elvis Presley balladeering out of the Lone Star State."

Hunter went on to call Strait "one of the two or three finest country singers of his generation."

How did it feel to be considered the savior of country music?

"It's a nice thing to have people say about you," Strait said, "but I don't know if it's really true. I feel that real country music and the audience for it was always there, but they weren't hearing it on the radio. Finally people got burned out on the crossover music that was played on country stations."

Strait was as humble and polite as ever when he said, "We've worked real hard. It's not as easy as people think—being out on the road as much as we are. But I'm real thankful to be doing this, because there's not a lot of people who get to experience this. There are a lot of singers and musicians out there, but there's not many of them that get to really experience the music business like we are right now.

"If you had asked me ten years ago, I would have said, 'I doubt I'll ever get this far, but hopefully someday, I'll get a record on the radio.' "

All the touring allowed Strait to win and bask in the adoration of thousands and thousands of fans, but at the same time he missed his family back home. Though it's possible for spouses, significant others, or even whole families to accompany stars on tour, it's not always as much fun as it might seem at first glance.

Even if the tour cities are places you'd like to visit, with interesting cultural or historical sites, great shopping, and outdoor spaces, you don't really have time to see anything. The show goes on until late at night, so you sleep late the next morning. By the time you're up, there's little left to the day. If there are press interviews or radio stations to visit, it's fun the first few times—but after a while it's all kind of the same.

"We've got two kids," Strait told an interviewer, explaining why Norma didn't go on the road very much. "During the school year, it's almost impossible for her to go 'cause my little boy is just fixing to turn five in May and he'll be starting preschool or kindergarten or whatever you call it next year. My daughter's thirteen, so she's got interests at home there, people that she wants to be with—her friends. So, she really doesn't care anything about going out on the road, plus she can't during the school year. I think we've adjusted as well as anybody can: it's working real good right now."

And so it was . . . until June 25, 1986, when a terrible tragedy struck the life of George Strait and his family: his daughter, Jenifer, was killed in a car accident south of San Marcos. She was thirteen years old and in the eighth grade.

Richard Mize, a regional staff writer for a Wichita Falls newspaper, was working as a country radio deejay in Sallisaw, Oklahoma, on the night of the accident. Some fans heard about the accident before he did. "I took call after call after call," he wrote, "from folks in eastern Oklahoma and western Arkansas who acted like Strait, a na-

56

168

tive of Pearsall, Texas, was one of their own. They shared his pain and his loss and their prayers."

Teenage girls not too much older than Jenifer called and cried on the phone. Mize writes, "Their 19-year-old deejay friend didn't know how to deal with it. I wept with them. . . . To many, George Strait the famous singer became George Strait the beloved friend."

It's easy to understand why he refused to give any interviews to the press for a full year after the tragedy.

Three weeks later, Strait was back on the road, burying himself in the relentless schedule of concerts that kept him busy through the fall. "A lot of people would have gone off in a lot of different ways after something like that happened," said his manager and friend Erv Woolsey. "But he didn't. George has his family and friends around him—and his belief in the Guy Up There. It was enough to get him through."

In August 1986, George Strait made his debut appearance in Great Britain at the Peterborough Festival of Country Music. It was the first time a "new" artist had headlined at this major event. Though he had never appeared onstage in England prior to this festival, George Strait was very popular in the United Kingdom.

He finished his dates in 1986 and even managed to get a Christmas album out—*Merry Christmas Strait to You*—for the 1986 holiday season. Then #7 became his next album to go gold.

After several months of silence, he began speaking to the press, but only under the condition that no one ask him about Jenifer.

Almost ten years later, Strait talked about the tragedy with Jack Hurst in an article printed in the *Austin American Statesman*. "When I lost my daughter . . . a lot of people of course wanted to talk and I didn't want to talk except to people I knew and cared about. Nothing worse could happen to a person and it made me kind of back away from doing a lot of interviews. I just decided, if my career suffers, it suffers."

Later he would say, "Early in my career, I had a very tragic thing happen. And I just realized that, you know, nothing could be worse than that. And so I'm gonna make these decisions and if they're right, they're right. If they're wrong, so be it. That's the way it's gonna be. And so, that's what I've done. I'm sure I may have made a lot of people mad, I don't know. But that's the way I chose to do it, and lucky for me it hasn't hurt my career any."

In October 1986, for the second time George Strait was named the Country Music Association's Top Male Vocalist, at the twentieth annual award show in Nashville. He dedicated the honor to the memory of his daughter.

As 1986 turned into 1987 Strait played a New Year's Eve concert at Dallas's Reunion Arena. This show was taped for a video called *George Strait Live*.

On January 6, 1987, tickets went on sale for

George Strait's appearances at the Houston Live-stock Show and Rodeo in late February at the Houston Astrodome. Within twenty-four hours, 112,808 tickets for a two-night engagement were sold out.

Later that month, Strait's new album, *Ocean Front Property*, made country music history by *entering* the Billboard country album chart at number one. It was the first time any album had ever debuted at the top of that chart.

Once again, Strait had created an album consisting of only ten cuts—ten exceptionally great cuts, of course—after an exhaustive search for songs. "He listens to so many songs, it's scary," says Erv Woolsey. "I just go look for them here and there," Strait says. "I go to publishing houses, people send me stuff. I look constantly for songs. We get tapes on the road a lot. I've got some people in Texas that I go through their stuff—some real good songwriters. We find 'em where I can get 'em."

George Strait's incredible record of number-one hits is unmatched in country music, and his track record of top-five and top-ten hit singles testifies to his relentless search for material and his unique touch for picking the right stuff. "Before I record, I probably listen to well over five hundred songs. You have to have a feel for it. I know when a song is right for me. It's really a process of elimination. You start going through all these tapes, play 'em again and again, and you keep at it until you got the very best ten or twelve songs that you can find."

The A&R department at MCA Records constantly sorts through the numerous songs that come in for George Strait. They mail demo tapes back and forth to Texas. Maybe for every hundred or so songs that are sent to him, Strait will like about twenty songs. "Whenever I get to Nashville," he says, "I've got a big box full to the top with tapes that I have to go through."

Ocean Front Property starts out with the humorous song "All My Ex's Live in Texas," written by Sanger D. Shafer and Lyndia J. Shafer. In the song, Rosanna from Texarkana, Eileen in Abilene, Alison in Galveston, and Dimples in Temple give Strait the chance to mention some more great Texas towns. He even throws in the Frio River, which is west and south of San Antonio. The song became yet another number-one single and was nominated for a Grammy.

The title cut, "Ocean Front Property," written by Dean Dillon, Hank Cochran, and Royce Porter, also hit the number-one spot. Royce Porter was quoted as saying it took the three writers a little more than an hour to create the song. According to ASCAP, it was the second-most-performed song in America in 1988. "Am I Blue?" written by David Chamberlain, was the album's other number-one hit.

Ocean Front Property has the distinction of being the first album on which the Ace in the Hole Band recorded with Strait on a major release. They played on "Hot Burning Flames" by Hank

Cochran, Mack Vickery, and Wayne Kemp, and "You Can't Buy Your Way Out of the Blues," written by Larry Cordle and Mike Anthony.

That a country album could sell so quickly and so well said something about the changing nature of the country music business. Back in the early eighties, after the success of the movie *Urban Cowboy*, country music records had risen in sales to over $250 million. Then they had plummeted down to $175 million. This was bad news for a city where country music is the third-largest industry. But by 1987, the news was better. And most of the improvement in sales was coming from the New Traditionalists. George Strait and others like him brought the sounds of pedal steel guitar, fiddle, and other old-time instruments back into country music.

In April of 1987, *The New York Times* published an article that said, "after a decade of slumping sales and stifled creativity, country music has turned itself around." Record companies were now reportedly looking hard to sign singers and songwriters whose music reflected the great honky tonk tradition of the forties and fifties.

Nashville's "songwriter bars," such as the famous Bluebird Café, were filled with aspiring stars hoping for two miracles: to pass the tough audition process that would allow them to play before an audience and to have their talents noticed by a record executive or manager. They were coming from all over the music world, including such bastions of rock and sophistication as New York, L.A., and London. One Nashville executive said that so many new and established songwriters were coming to Music City that it had become a new Tin Pan Alley, New York's famous former songwriting hub.

A 1993 movie, *The Thing Called Love*, directed by the well-known Peter Bogdanovich, painted a realistic picture of what it's like for all those aspiring writers and singers who come to Nashville. River Phoenix, Samantha Mathis, and Sandra Bullock starred in the movie, which was filmed in part in the real Bluebird Café on Hillsboro Road in Nashville. Trisha Yearwood has a small role in the picture playing herself.

When George Strait decided to play the Las Vegas Hilton in 1987, he probably wasn't looking to make history, just music. But Strait became the only artist besides Elvis Presley to sell out his debut engagement at what was then the largest hotel in the world.

That accomplishment caught the attention of Colonel Tom Parker, Elvis's longtime manager and mentor, who was a consultant to the Hilton Hotels chain. Colonel Parker often came backstage wearing his "George Strait" Resistol cowboy hat just to chat with the singer.

"He's got some great stories about different dates and places they played," Strait said. "For my last birthday he had the governor of Tennessee make me an honorary colonel, so now when he writes me he writes 'Colonel George Strait.' "

Colonel Tom Parker believed "Colonel" George Strait would go on to be an even bigger star than he already was. He also thought Strait had talents beyond his music.

As for Las Vegas, Strait continued to be a huge draw for all the partygoers and vacationers in one of the most fun places in America. "Out here, you really gotta pace yourself," he said. "Especially if you're like me and you like to go out and take part in what Las Vegas has to offer. If you don't, you'll wear yourself out."

Strait also played Lake Tahoe, that breathtaking resort area that straddles the California and Nevada border with a lake so clear and blue you just thank the Lord you've had the chance to see it. When he debuted at Caesar's Tahoe Casino in June 1988, the audience no doubt thanked the Lord they'd had the chance to see him.

"Anyone lucky enough to see and hear George Strait in the late 1980s," journalist Bob Allen wrote in *Country Music* magazine, "is seeing and hearing state of the art country music at its best."

John Lomax wrote in *Honky Tonk* magazine, "Texas has yielded the finest honky tonk singers this country has ever known and now the Lone Star State has produced another who is likely to be around as long as there are juke boxes, tight country quintets, good old girls and hell-raising cowboys."

Beginning in 1987, Strait cut his touring down from well over two hundred to about seventy-five dates a year. Touring less only made his fans want him more. This meant playing bigger and bigger venues.

George Strait's concerts always received great reviews. Critics and fans alike commented on his no-frills showmanship that made the music, not the special effects, the star of the show. Strait's stage has always been simple. It looked no different than if the band were playing in a small dance hall in the 1940s. The only concession to modern times was the big video screens scattered throughout the arenas. These brought the fans even closer than if they'd been sitting in the front row and now gave everyone a new relationship with their favorite country star.

The use of the screens also meant that women all over the arenas, even way up in the balcony, were having heart palpitations over George Strait. "It's a genuine crime," one reviewer said, "that one man got a double dose of talent and handsomeness."

For a reportedly shy and reserved guy, he sure seemed to enjoy all the wild adulation his shows inspired. Strait says he doesn't mind at all when the fans get close.

At a show in Austin, for example, a girl leaped onto the stage. "I mean, she grabbed me," Strait said. "She had her arms and legs around me and she didn't want to let go. I didn't think we were ever going to get her loose." He couldn't even pretend to keep singing. "She had me," he says. "I couldn't even get to the mike."

Strait said he knows some stars find this sort of thing unnerving, but it doesn't scare him or make him angry. "I like it that people get that excited by the music," he says. "I don't mind. I'm like any other musician, insofar as I feed off that kind of energy."

But make no mistake about it, George Strait has always been a devoted husband and family man in real life. "I try not to take it too seriously when people say things about the sex-symbol thing," he said. "That might be something that happens onstage, but . . . that's not me."

George Strait: Greatest Hits Volume Two was released by MCA Records in September 1987. During this time, George Strait and Jimmy Bowen were at work producing another album.

Each new album represented an enormous task. "I'm really serious about my music. Every time I go in the studio to make a new record, I get nervous because I want it to be my best ever," says the man who's never made a bad album. "Not really different, just better, because I hope to be doing this same thing for years to come."

Strait's eleventh album, like all the others, would be recorded in Nashville, but as soon as it was finished, he'd be back in Texas. Some people thought his haste to leave the town stemmed from the resentment he still felt at having been dismissed in the 1970s. Perhaps a more accurate reason is that he had no privacy or real life in Nashville. Wherever he went, he'd get bombarded by songwriters wanting to pitch him their songs. And the thousands of fans who pour into Nashville year-round, even when no Fan Fair or CMA week is scheduled, are thrilled to death to see a star on the street. Strait was always being hit up for autographs.

Then there were the women who thought he was gorgeous. If he had an appointment to visit his record company or a publishing company, all the women employees would be in a state of excitement for days before he was due in. His actual arrival would send them into a frenzy.

Strait's desire to stay in Texas is just the natural inclination of a man who loves his home and the life he has there. He loves rodeo events, of which there sure are a lot more in Texas than in Nashville. He does a lot of deer hunting. He loves the simple life he was born and raised in.

Coproducing the albums with Jimmy Bowen fit in perfectly with his life. "It's funny the way we coproduce an album," he said, "because I don't think anybody else does it quite like this. I go in the studio and I can do my part in four or five days—cut the basic tracks, do my vocals. Then we'll go over the different songs, and we'll decide where we want harmony parts, and how many, and this and that. And I'll go on home to Texas or whatever, and [Bowen] will go back in the studio and do 'em.

"Then he'll send me all these cassette tapes of

what he's done, and I'll listen to them and call him up and say yes to this, or no to that, or 'This sounds great,' or 'Let's change this to that,' or 'Let's cut this part out.' Jimmy will go back in the studio and make all the changes, then send me another cassette of it to listen to. He'll send me maybe twenty cassettes before we finally get through."

Bowen writes in *Rough Mix*, "I'd send George a rough mix on the road and he literally phoned it in: he'd sit with a lyric sheet identical to mine and tell me just where in the tracks he wanted harmonies dubbed and whether he heard two- or three-part harmony."

For an album of ten songs, sometimes twelve or thirteen are recorded. A record-company staffer takes the demos of the song and makes lyric sheets with chord notations for all the players. Each musician then uses these to prepare for the sessions.

Songs worth considering might come in to Erv Woolsey or MCA's A&R department as late as the week of the recording sessions. Especially with George Strait, the studio's song list was subject to change at any minute. "Even all the way through the recording session itself, I'm still looking for songs," he says. "If I find one that's better than the one I brought in the recording studio with me that day, I'll do the new one."

This is why songwriters can get crazy sometimes. Even after they're told their song has been chosen and even after it is recorded in the studio, there's no guarantee it will show up on an album. Most artists and producers would subscribe to what Strait says: "You never know until you get in there and start working on it." Songs have been cut after all the music has been mixed and a master tape is ready. They have been cut after the record company has asked the music publisher for "label copy"—the exact, correct names of the writers and publishers to be included in the album notes. You can't ever be sure. Although CDs have replaced LPs, the old saying is still true: "It's not final till it's vinyl."

"I have always gone into the studio to make it better than the last one," Strait said about the process of recording a new album. "Each time I think I have."

The album *If You Ain't Lovin', You Ain't Livin'* was released in February 1988 and went gold within two months.

At around the same time, the video *George Strait—Live* hit the marketplace. The New Year's Eve show at the Dallas Reunion Arena that had been taped a year before went gold six months later. For a video that means selling over fifty thousand copies—although at the time of this writing, the total is up to over two hundred thousand copies. It is one of the all-time best-selling country music videos.

Strait was hot in every way a singer can be. His albums were selling through the roof. His first major video release was an almost instant classic.

His ticket sales topped $10 million, making him and the Ace in the Hole Band the highest-grossing country act on the road. And radio was just loving him. George Strait was now a bigger star than he'd ever dreamed he'd be.

It became a kind of truism in the country music business that George Strait and the New Traditionalists had revived Nashville by returning country music to its roots. By bringing traditional country, and other kinds of traditional music, to Nashville, they were also responsible for carrying Music City into a golden future. Record companies were using the income from increased album sales to improve technical quality, and with better equipment, production values improved as well. The new artists also had a profound effect on country radio, which had for years been geared to an aging audience that loved the music but didn't buy records. Now radio was following the tastes of the new listeners, who wanted to hear the newer acts.

There was plenty of debate in the late 1980s about New Traditionalist versus old country, pop influence on country, and even country influence on pop. Through it all, George Strait just kept making the music he wanted to make, the way he wanted to make it. The fact that some people felt his music was the cornerstone of a revolution in Nashville was a source of some amusement to an artist who was just keepin' it country.

* * *

If You Ain't Lovin', You Ain't Livin' produced three more number-one singles. The warm and touching ballad "Famous Last Words of a Fool," written by Dean Dillon and Rex Houston, was a song Strait had passed on once but decided to include on this album. The title track, "If You Ain't Lovin', You Ain't Livin'," written by Tommy Collins, is a cover of Texas honky tonker Faron Young's hit from 1954. It was one of the tracks Strait had recorded for the album he scrapped before producing *Does Fort Worth Ever Cross Your Mind.*

"Baby Blue" is the first of many Aaron Barker songs Strait recorded, and it was something of a miracle that he recorded it at all. According to *The Tennessean,* Barker had given a demo of his songs to a friend, who gave it to a publisher in Hondo, Texas, who accidentally brought it on a song-plugging trip to Nashville. Strait liked the song a lot. The only problem was that the tape's label identified the songwriter only as "Aaron." Erv Woolsey managed to track down the song-writer, and the rest is hit-record history.

The Orlando Sentinel said in its review of the album, "He may not be a songwriter, but Strait is one of the best song-pickers in the field. Of the ten tunes on *If You Ain't Lovin', You Ain't Livin',* eight are choice cuts—and even the other two are above average."

The Academy of Country Music, which had made George Strait its Top Vocalist of the Year in

1984 and 1985, had given that honor to Randy
Travis for the next two years. In 1988, they returned the crown to Strait.

Both men were on the bill that year for the
Marlboro Country Music Tour, with their megastar colleagues Alabama and the Judds. It included a four-hour marathon for the most urban
of cowboys and cowgirls in New York's Madison
Square Garden on May 21.

"New York City went wild over country music,"
Strait said.

Now his band was almost as big an attraction
as he was. Critics and fans couldn't get enough of
what some have called the tightest band onstage,
the Ace in the Hole Band.

"I love their big-band sound," Strait says. "You
get such a full sound up onstage with that many
players. If I could, I'd add more—a third fiddle
player, probably a mandolin player, and maybe
even some horns."

Later that year, George Strait found time to relax and enjoy his family and home. He makes no
secret that one of the things he likes to do back in
Texas is go deer hunting. On Thanksgiving Day,
1988, he bagged a whitetail of possible record-
book size. Game warden Larry Griffin in Cotulla,
Texas, and LaSalle County sheriff Darwin Avant
confirmed that George Strait shot a buck with
thirteen-point antlers, a matched set of six on
each main beam, with one other partial point
on one side. The rack measured eighteen inches

across. He shot the deer on his ranch in Webb County, about sixty miles southwest of San Antonio. The deer was expected to produce a preliminary score of at least 191 on the Boone and Crockett scale used to evaluate trophy racks.

Strait's February 1989 album, *Beyond the Blue Neon*, contains a tribute to the Ace in the Hole Band. Though it is not really about them, one of the songs is called "Ace in the Hole," by Dennis Adkins.

Strait had often been given songs with this title, but since he regarded the band as the best in the world, a song that used its name had to be one that really knocked him out. This one had just the right combination of swing music and sassy lyrics. Ironically, although the Ace in the Hole Band performed the song live and still does so, and always to great applause, the album version was cut in the studio by the usual studio musicians.

His twelfth album, *Beyond the Blue Neon*, received lots of praise from many quarters for its smooth vocals, its continued exploration of the possibilities of Western swing, its Sinatra-like touches, and more complex instrumentation.

"I went into the studio with a sax player this time—not for a saxophone solo, which you won't hear on the album, but just to beef it up a little," Strait said. "We did that on some of the songs, and I think it worked really well."

* * *

There's a lot you can do when you're feeling totally confident and at the top of your game. The world of music had come to accept George Strait on his own terms by now. But the best review the latest album got was from the man himself. George Strait said, "I think *Beyond the Blue Neon* is the best I've ever done. I felt . . . like I'd accomplished something that I wanted to accomplish for a long, long time."

Many critics and fans count this album among their favorites. Strait himself enjoyed making it. "You can go into the studio and pretty much tell how things are going by the way the musicians were really enjoying themselves," he said.

There's more than a little heartache in this album. "Baby's Gotten Good at Goodbye," written by Tony and Troy Martin, is another twist on the breaking-up song. Here, a man is worried that his woman may not come back this time. She's left him before, but this time, when she looked back, there were no tears in her eyes.

When it came time to select the singles from *Beyond the Blue Neon*, Strait said, "The material is really strong, and I'm having a hard time choosing singles, because I like every song on the album—and that's kind of unusual. You start out that way, normally, and when you get finished, there's always a few that stand out."

In the end, he made the right choices. *Blue Neon* charted five singles: "Baby's Gotten Good at Goodbye," "Ace in the Hole," "Overnight Success" (written by Sanger D. Shafer), "Hollywood

Squares" (written by Wayland Patton, Larry Cordle, and Jeff Tanguay), and "What's Going On in Your World?" written by David Chamberlain and Royce Porter.

David Chamberlain and Royce Porter said the inspiration for their song was a real-life event: one of them walked into a studio one day and said "good morning" to someone and that person replied, "What's happening in your world?" It became ASCAP's Song of the Year in 1990.

"Hollywood Squares" is another of the humorous songs that seem to work so well for George Strait. It's the story of a guy who has so many ex-wives and owes so much money that he thinks he belongs on the game show.

The *Los Angeles Times* called *Beyond the Blue Neon* "the best album [Strait]'s ever made." And David Zimmerman, music critic for *USA Today*, included it on his list of 1989's ten best albums in all categories.

At a party in Houston to celebrate the album's release, Bob Wills's widow, Betty, presented Strait with the hat that Wills had worn onstage during his performing career.

"It's something that I'll keep and pass down to my son," George said. "For her to think of me and my music and to give me something like that of his means so much to me."

In April of 1989, the Academy of Country Music once again named George Strait the Top Vocalist of the Year. The accolades kept coming.

* * *

George Strait was walking down a corridor in the White House with his wife, Norma, and son, Bubba. "I was pretty overwhelmed by all the things around me, the history," he later said. "You walk down the hall and see huge paintings and bronzes of Lincoln and Washington."

The Straits were at the White House in September of 1989 for a ceremony in the Rose Garden. Another famous "George" from Texas, President George Bush, was honoring Strait and eleven others with the American Vocation Success Award. Top fashion designer Norma Kamale and space shuttle commander Major General Joe Henry Engle were among the honorees. Strait was the only entertainer to receive the honor that day.

"The award really meant a lot, especially coming from the president," he said. Referring to the fact that he had taken vocational agriculture in high school, he said, "I hope it can serve as an inspiration for some kids out there in high school and even younger that the 4H and FFA [Future Farmers of America] are really good for young kids. I was in FFA in high school. It taught me a whole lot."

After the ceremony, President Bush invited the Strait family into the Oval Office.

"He really and truly is a country music fan," Strait said. "He took us back into his private office where they built him a special desk with built-in speakers. He put on some country music for us."

President Bush wrote a note to George Jr.'s teacher excusing him from classes. After his son brought the note to school, "We asked the teacher to give it back to us," Strait said.

"The president asked, 'When are you going to come play for us at the White House?' I said, 'Just ask me.' "

The next day, Erv Woolsey called the White House to make arrangements.

Entertainer of the Year. That award is the highest accolade a performer can receive from the Country Music Association. And it's one that eluded George Strait for four years, arguably the four most successful years of his career to date.

He was nominated in 1985. Again in 1986 and 1987. For a fourth consecutive time in 1988.

When he didn't win, he said, "You try not to get excited or disappointed about these awards. But that night, I really wanted to win that thing. Being nominated for several years and coming away empty-handed was kind of discouraging." Still, as he told the *Tulsa Tribune*, when fans "buy your records, you know you've gotten a bigger vote than you could get at any awards show."

When the 1989 CMA nominations were announced, no one was surprised that the list of nominees for Entertainer of the Year once again included the name of George Strait. The others were Hank Williams, Jr., Randy Travis, Reba

McEntire, and Ricky Van Shelton. No, it was no surprise that he was nominated again, but no one expected him to win.

Many nominees for awards lobby for themselves and put themselves at the center of public-relations and advertising campaigns carefully orchestrated by their record companies and publicity firms. George Strait didn't do this. After the nomination, he kept a low profile, a habit he conceded had "probably hurt my career a little. But that's the way I've been ever since I started singing," he said. "I've always found it hard to talk about myself, I don't know why but it's hard for me to do. I'm a private person. I don't mind talking about some things, but there are other things I feel like are nobody's business but mine.

"I think everybody's that way, really, but if you're an entertainer, people want to know every little thing there is to know and—hey—I'm just a human being like everybody else. I have things that are private."

Norma told him she was sure he would win this year, but, he says, "I didn't believe her." All he would say before the awards was, "They're great when you win. When you don't win, it's like, 'Ah, awards. They don't mean anything.' "

Barbara Mandrell was the presenter of the award that year. When she opened the envelope to read the name of the winner, she gasped, "George Strait!"

"I really wanted that thing," Strait said, "and I was just about to think that it was gonna slip by me. It just knocked me out when they called my name!"

Knocked him out so much that he just sat there for a second before climbing onto the stage. He looked down at the envelope Mandrell handed him and said, "Let me read that again." After confirming the fact that it was indeed his name on the piece of paper, he held up the crystal trophy in his hands and said, "I'm so excited. . . . I want to thank my great band, and MCA records for signing me, and my wife, Norma, and I'd like to say hi back home to Bubba—or George Jr., as he likes to be called now."

Later, as fans offered him their congratulations, he joked, "Slap me! Pinch me!"

"I've worked really hard for eight years," he said. "It finally paid off."

He told *USA Today* he almost felt like crying.

Strait was told that no members of the local press had predicted his win. "Well, I'm glad I proved them wrong," he said with a grin. "It makes me feel proud 'cause I know I've got fans out there and I know that they enjoy the shows, because I can tell when we're out playin'."

Five nominations had been honors in themselves, but nothing beats a win. "I was surprised and in a way relieved that it had finally happened, not just for me, but the guys in my band," Strait said, "and everyone that has worked so hard with me over the years."

The cover of George Strait's next album featured him in a tuxedo, black cowboy hat, and

shiny belt buckle engraved with the words CMA
ENTERTAINER OF THE YEAR.

"If I never win it again, I really don't care," he
said. "I've won it once and that was the icing on
the cake. It meant a lot to achieve that."

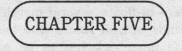

CHAPTER FIVE

Star Quality

George Strait starred in the movie *Pure Country* as a country singer who decided to walk away from the music business after his success had become more than he could handle.

Lucky for Strait's real-life fans, it was just a movie.

Few people ever know what it's like to become legends. Fewer still become legends in their own time. But George Strait did just that as he continued to make great country music in the early 1990s.

It was a long-standing tradition for fans to go wild for George Strait at the Houston Livestock Show and Rodeo. The fifty-eighth annual show in 1990 was no exception. A Texas-size and Texas-style party, the Livestock Show and Rodeo was an eighteen-day extravaganza that attracted hundreds of thousands of visitors from all over the U.S.A. and around the world each year.

Kicking off the whole thing on Saturday, February 17, was the Downtown Rodeo Parade. It

began at the corner of—where else?—Texas Street
and continued along twenty-four city blocks, featuring dozens of floats, several marching bands,
and thousands of trail riders who had traveled
for days on horseback just to be part of the
spectacle.

This was followed by the World Championship
Bar-B-Que Contest, which attracted cooks from
all over the state, a fiddler's competition, a hay-
hauling contest, a game of horseshoes, and even
a quilting contest. The livestock show featured
horses, donkeys, mules, sheep, rabbits, goats,
cattle, and even llamas brought in by breeders
and ranchers from thirty-five states. At night the
Rodeo Fireworks Spectacular, choreographed to
country music, gave folks something to talk about
for days afterward.

The Houston Livestock Show and Rodeo raised
more than $3 million to help more than a thou-
sand Texas students pay for college. Not to mention the estimated $70 million that it pumped each
year into the local economy. The very best in
country music was one of its biggest attractions.
George Strait was at the top of an all-star lineup
of twenty-seven acts set to appear in the Astrodome. Also on the schedule were the Judds,
Ricky Van Shelton, Alabama, and Clint Black.

Strait has a special place in his heart for the
Houston Livestock Show and Rodeo, and no matter how much he cuts back on his touring, it's unlikely he'll ever skip this event.

The first time he played it was back in 1981,

when he received a last-minute call asking him to fill in for an ill Eddie Rabbitt. Fifty thousand fans were waiting for some great music and the concert promoters didn't want to disappoint them. They sent a private plane to Austin to pick up Strait and the Ace in the Hole Band.

At the time, many of the people in the audience didn't know who George Strait was. But then he started playing. He and the band put all they had into the performance of their best songs. After they were through, Strait further impressed—no, make that shocked—the crowd by jumping on a horse and riding around the arena. Then he threw his hat to the fans and rode off.

He's been throwing his hat to the crowd after his shows ever since.

Now, on a Wednesday and Thursday in February 1990, audiences were treated to two more wonderful shows by the CMA's reigning Entertainer of the Year. Every George Strait show is great, but when he plays the Livestock Show and Rodeo, he doesn't just keep it country, he keeps it *Texas*. The emphasis on Texas dance-hall music also showcases the Ace in the Hole Band at their best, right there in their home state.

Once again, Houston had a blast!

At the Academy of Country Music's April awards-show presentation, broadcast on national TV, George Strait was the host along with singer K. T. Oslin and one of the stars of the TV show *Dallas*, Patrick Duffy.

Strait sang the first single from his new album, *Livin' It Up*. The song was "Love Without End, Amen," written by Aaron Baker. A story of the uncompromising and unconditional love that a father feels for his son, it became an instant favorite—as well as Strait's biggest hit to date. It went to number one on the *Billboard* charts and stayed there for an incredible five weeks, the longest any country song had spent on top since Dolly Parton's "Here You Come Again" in 1977. The song has become classic George Strait.

Livin' It Up was coproduced by Jimmy Bowen, even though he had left MCA the previous winter. Many critics called it Strait's best album yet.

To create *Livin' It Up*, he once again searched for and found the best songwriters around. This album included songs written by all-time greats Harlan Howard, Conway Twitty, and Carl Perkins, as well as Dean Dillon, Buddy Cannon, Bill Mack, and Clay Blaker, from San Marcos, Texas.

"Drinking Champagne" was written by Bill Mack, who would become famous six years later as the writer of LeAnn Rimes's smash debut single, "Blue." "Drinking Champagne" became a number-four hit. "I've Come To Expect It from You," written by Dean Dillon and Buddy Cannon, made it to number one, and stayed there for five weeks. It was Strait's twentieth number-one hit. The Ace in the Hole Band backed him on two songs on the album—Harlan Howard's "Someone Had to Teach You" and Conway Twitty's "She Loves Me (She Don't Love You)."

After the acclaim of *Beyond the Blue Neon*, *Livin' It Up* shipped gold. That means it had advance orders of more than the 500,000 copies it needed to sell to achieve gold record status.

Livin' It Up is the album that featured George Strait on the cover proudly wearing the belt buckle that proclaimed him 1989's CMA Entertainer of the Year. What a great outfit: a black tuxedo jacket, white formal shirt, and a great pair of jeans.

The summer concert season was on again. And, as reliably as the sun rose and set on the Texas flatlands, the fans were out in force. Many would stand in line for hours as soon as the ticket sales were announced. The truly devoted fans were following Strait from show to show. They would drive miles just to hear another dose of Strait's brand of country music.

George Strait continued to finish his shows by throwing his hat out into the crowd. Not since the heaviest rock acts had smashed their guitars onstage had there been such roars of excitement.

Like fans of all the big country stars as well as their rock-and-roll counterparts, George Strait fans were spending a ton of money on merchandise: the T-shirts, jackets, calendars, photos, and other treasures featuring his picture and his name.

Guys were coming to the shows dressed like George Strait, in pressed jeans, starched button-down shirts, and cowboy hats. The women wore rhinestones, fringe, and leather. The women were also getting bolder, making no bones about how attractive they thought George Strait was.

WHAT DO WOMEN LOVE ABOUT GEORGE STRAIT?

"He's a Texas boy and we like the fact, naturally, that he's gorgeous."

"He's sooooo cute."

"When he sings a song, he's singing it right at you."

"He's fine."

"He's clean-cut. That's the most important thing, and the fact that he's a Texan."

"He's easy to identify with. He's real."

"His eyes."

"He's got a smooth, sexy, beautiful voice."

"His looks."

"He looks great in his Wranglers."

"His buckskin ropers."

"He's soft about everything and he's sweet."

"He's just all man."

WHAT DO THE MEN SAY?

One husband said about his wife's
high esteem for George Strait:
"I don't mind. At first, I said,
'Hey,' but now I don't care."

Another guy said:
"He's a pretty clean-cut guy, a sharp-looking
guy. He seems like he'd be all right to talk to."

What did George Strait think of all the attention?
"I don't take it all that serious," he said. "It's a
fun thing when I'm onstage, but when I'm offstage it's different. The looks and all that stuff is
pretty secondary. The bottom line is if you don't
have good material, you're just another Joe Blow
walkin' onstage."

In the midst of all this George Strait mania, *People* named him one of the magazine's 50 Most Beautiful People.

There he is in a super full-page, full-color photo by photographer P. F. Bentley, wearing a red-and-white-striped shirt, pressed blue jeans, black boots, and his CMA Entertainer of the Year belt buckle. Of course, he's wearing his white Resistol hat. In Strait's white-gloved right hand is a lariat. In the background is a white horse with a sharp brown leather saddle.

The caption says: "Upstanding, heart-tugging country and western balladeer and fourth generation Texan; 37. Hitched to high school honey Norma." George Strait's quote says, "It's very important for a country star to be able to sing. Anything else, like looks, is pretty secondary."

Among the great things about George Strait is that he really is the nice guy he appears to be, with the decent values that he appears to have. Unlike a lot of other famous people, he has a grip on the difference between real life and the entertainment business. He wants to sing and make music and there's no question he loves being onstage. But when he puts down his guitar and goes back home, he has another life, a real life with family, friends, and interests that keep him just as happy, if not a little happier, than his show-business life. Men and women alike admire this genuineness in him.

As Michael Spies wrote in the *Houston Chronicle*,

"Women can't believe that someone who looks this good sounds this good and men can't believe a guy who sounds this good has the luck to look this good."

Strait has discussed his feelings about the women who fling themselves at him while he's touring and its relationship to his marriage. "It concerned us both," he said, referring to Norma. "There I am out on the road miles away where there are plenty of women, while the only woman in my life is home in Texas. But Norma was very supportive, and this success is something she always wanted for me because she knew I wanted it so bad.

"We've learned to cope with the fact that the George Strait onstage is an image. And the one at home with my wife and Bubba is a family-loving man. You've got to keep the stage world and your real world separated or you're headed for trouble. In other words, you can't live out the songs you sing."

That's one of the things the fans like about him, that a man so good-looking and appealing is still married and faithful to his high-school sweetheart. "Well, I'm definitely no ladies' man," he said. "I'm happy women fans like me. I appreciate all my fans."

One evening when George Strait was on-stage doing his show at the Star Lake Amphitheater in

Pittsburgh, Pennsylvania, the most outrageous woman in country music suddenly strutted out from the wings, sauntered across the stage, and plucked his hat right off his head.

Then she plunked it down on her own.

Right into the microphone, in her trademark sexy voice, she said, "Can we do something together?"

The place went wild as George Strait and Tanya Tucker sang a sensational duet of "Amarillo by Morning."

August brought the Country Music Association Awards nominations around again, and again George Strait was nominated for Entertainer of the Year.

Did he want to win for a second time?

"Heck, yeah," he said, "but that's almost too much to ask for."

Well, guess what? For the second consecutive year, George Strait was named Entertainer of the Year.

"I'm truly speechless," he said.

Backstage after the ceremonies, he had a little more to say. "It's a real boost, I'll tell you. It really gives you a lot of motivation."

Chill of an Early Fall, released in March of 1991, is considered one of his best albums ever. Alanna Nash in *Entertainment Weekly* called it "the album George Strait was born to make . . . a sublime refinement of all the ballads, honky tonk and hot Texas dance music he's done before." She went on to say, "Through hard work, he's made the most of his talents and become a modern master."

Once again, Strait had worked hard to select his material. He started work on the album with a great bunch, but, as he said, "You never know until you get in there and start working on it."

"If I Know Me," by Dean Dillon and Pam Belford, and "You Know Me Better Than That," by Tony Haselden and Anna Lisa Graham, both hit number one. The title track, "Chill of an Early Fall," went to number three. In an interview in *Country Song Roundup*, the husband-and-wife songwriting team Green Daniel and Gretchen Peters talked about how their song became a George Strait hit.

First, Curtis Wright, a new Capitol Records artist, sang it during a showcase of his talents. It was heard by another artist, Joe Barnhill, who included it on his album for Universal Records. It was a good cut on a good but not hugely successful album. During all this time, however, the song was in the pile of what the songwriters called "the seven thousand songs" people submitted to George Strait.

When Jimmy Bowen heard the song, he thought it would be great for George. Erv Woolsey heard it and agreed. The song tells a deeply emotional story of a man who isn't happy about his lady's visits from an old lover. He's anticipating heartbreak sooner or later, just as in the fall one anticipates an imminent storm. By the time George Strait heard "Chill of an Early Fall," he was near the end of recording the album. Including it was another eleventh-hour decision.

Gretchen Peters told *Country Song Roundup*, " 'Chill' went to the top of the list. I know they worked all day cutting it. I was floored when I found out George Strait had cut it. Then the next thing is, it's the title cut. I was floored, then floored again when I found out it was the single."

The Ace in the Hole Band was showcased on three consecutive cuts on the album: "Home in San Antone," "Milkcow Blues," and "Lovesick Blues."

"George has a lot of friends where he lives," says Erv Woolsey. "They're not in the music business. I think if he made a record that they didn't like, they'd let him know."

George Strait played a concert at San Antonio's Sea World in July 1991. As usual, he had the crowd in a frenzy. "This is the shortest I've had to drive for a show in a long time," he said, "and I like it."

"I love George Strait," said one fan. "He's right up there with Elvis."

Like Elvis, Strait has a huge entourage when he performs. At the Sea World show, there were more than twenty-two cars, four tour buses, and one stretch limo.

Another fan had traveled to the concert from

Florence, Mississippi. It was the seventy-sixth George Strait concert she had attended.

Much has been written about the effects of bar coding, those black-and-white lines that have found their way onto the packages of everything from appliances to bubble gum, on the measurement of album sales. In the early nineties, SoundScan, a company from Hartsdale, New York, had shown the record business a new way to tally sales using these codes. Not only would stores and record companies have access to this sales information, it would also provide the data for the documents on which the music business lives and dies: the *Billboard* charts.

No longer was country music a distant cousin or, more accurately, a poor relation of the music business. Now it was clear that huge numbers of people were really forking over their hard-earned dollars to buy the kind of straight-from-the-heartland music that many of the so-called experts had looked down their noses at. As it turned out, country music chart toppers weren't just beating out the competition in their own category; they were showing that they formed a nice healthy chunk of the music business's overall pie.

While George Strait's numbers were even more evident than before, the really big news was the arrival on the scene of such artists as Clint Black and Alan Jackson. Although both of these singers had obviously paid their dues, it suddenly seemed as if they had just come out of nowhere and hit the charts at the top.

Black had been born in New Jersey but his family moved to Houston when he was just three months old. He started songwriting at the age of fifteen, and by the early nineties, he had been playing in Houston clubs for ten years. His first album, *Killin' Time*, was released in 1989. His first single, "A Better Man," went number one.

Alan Jackson had started playing with a country band in Georgia at the age of twenty and moved to Nashville in 1985. He sang demos and was a staff songwriter with Glen Campbell Music. *Here in the Real World* was his first album. In March of 1991, a year after its release, it went platinum.

Black, Jackson, and others like them were the next new breed of country musicians. They played traditional country music, honky tonk tunes, and added some pop touches. They were young and handsome. They wore nice shirts, clean jeans, sharp boots, and cowboy hats. Instantly they were dubbed the "hat acts."

If SoundScan brought a new awareness of Nashville's rising profile in the overall music business and called attention to the success of Black and Jackson, it made the rise of Garth Brooks seem nothing short of phenomenal. Brooks was getting hot in 1990 and 1991. Through a combination of undeniable talent, stellar marketing, and that essential ingredient in all showbiz success—timing—the young man from Oklahoma was riding high on the charts.

Garth Brooks had played in local clubs in Stillwater, Oklahoma, while attending Oklahoma State University, where he majored in advertising. He had come to Nashville in 1985 but stayed less than twenty-four hours after realizing what a hard road he'd have to travel to get noticed. Two years later he came back to town. After showing the extraordinary power of his singing voice on demos, he landed a record deal with Capital Records.

His first album, entitled *Garth Brooks*, came out in 1989. The first single "Much Too Young (to Feel This Damn Old)," reached the top ten. The next single, "If Tomorrow Never Comes," went to number one. More hits followed, including one of the most popular ever, "Friends in Low Places," written by Dewayne Blackwell and Earl Bud Lee.

Garth's second album, *No Fences*, released in September of 1990, stayed on the top of the country album chart for an amazing twenty-three weeks. It also reached number twelve on the pop-album chart. By September of 1993, these two albums would sell a combined *15 million copies*. No fooling. It was measured by SoundScan.

Now, Clint Black, Alan Jackson, and Garth Brooks have something besides country music in common: they all admit they owe their success in large measure to George Strait. Strait's accomplishment in turning country music back to its roots and his string of number-one hits from

1981 to 1989 had paved the way for these new stars.

Asked how he felt about people citing him as an influence, Strait said, "Well, that's awful nice. It's a nice compliment and I'm glad to know that my music has meant something to people and maybe it's influenced a few people, I don't know."

Was having younger guys give him credit for their own success a kind of backhanded compliment? Did it mean George Strait should go out to pasture?

"I had never really thought about it," Strait says, "being an influence on somebody's career. I thought, 'Well, I haven't been around near long enough to do that.' But evidently I had. But it kind of took me by surprise, and I didn't really know how to take it at first. But after I thought about it, it's quite a compliment to be looked at like that. Because I had people that I looked up to when I was starting out and coming along, and I guess everybody has those."

Of the three, Garth Brooks was the most vocal about Strait's inspiration. When he was honored with the 1991 ACM award as Male Vocalist of the Year, he said, "I'm very happy but I'm a little embarrassed. I just want Mr. Strait to know he's always my male vocalist."

While George Strait continued to produce hits in 1990 and 1991, these other guys' songs were getting into the top five. No one necessarily saw all this as a competition: after all, Black, Jackson, Brooks, and Strait were all winners in the game of the radio and sales charts. Yes, Strait's album sales took a dip during 1991 and 1992, but a dip from the heights he was at still meant big sales. For his part, Strait just continued making the music he'd always made. He wasn't an artist who had ever worried about trends. He wasn't about to start worrying now.

"Nobody puts any pressure on me about material," he says. "I'm sure that if I took a real rotten song into the studio, Jimmy Bowen wouldn't hesitate to tell me not to do it. I'd listen to him, too—I trust his taste—but it hasn't ever happened."

Strait had been a star for ten years, a long time for a performer in the last quarter of the twentieth century. He had come to Nashville determined to do it his way, and up to now, that's exactly what he'd done. That's the way he'd keep on doing it.

In December of 1991 MCA Records released the third George Strait greatest hits collection in ten years. The album was called *Ten Strait Hits*.

At the time, Strait and Jimmy Bowen were producing their last album together. Bowen had been producing Strait's albums even after he left MCA Records to go over to lead Capitol Records' Nashville division.

"Bowen is one of the best producers of country, or any other kind of music, in the world," Strait said. Together, the two had produced a total of eleven albums, with music that will live on as classic listening for decades to come.

Holding My Own was released in April 1992. The album's two singles "Gone As a Girl Can Get," written by Jerry Max Lane, and "So Much Like My Dad," by Chips Moman and Bobby Emmons, went to number five but no higher. *Holding My Own* seemed to get lost in the shuffle. That was because there was something new and very exciting going on in the world of George Strait.

"The hardest part of all this is being treated like a star," George Strait said. "It's sometimes hard for me to deal with it. I love my fans, I really do. But, ya know, it's hard for me to take bein' treated that way."

Maybe that's why it had taken five years to agree to the idea Colonel Tom Parker, Elvis Presley's longtime manager, had been advocating ever since he'd met Strait at the Las Vegas Hilton in 1987. In addition to being wowed by Strait's ability to sell out his debut engagement there—an accomplishment only equaled by Elvis Presley himself—Parker was convinced that George Strait should make a movie.

Other country stars had made movies. No one can forget Dolly Parton in *9 to 5*, *Steel Magnolias*, and *The Best Little Whorehouse in Texas*—the movie for which she wrote the megahit "I Will Always Love You." Kris Kristofferson had done a raft of films, including *Blume in Love*, *Pat Garrett and Billy the Kid*, and *A Star Is Born* opposite Barbra Streisand. Kenny Rogers made his mark in the many *Gambler* movies. Willie Nelson had done a bunch himself, including *Electric Horseman* and *Stagecoach*. Rock stars like David Bowie and Mick Jagger were also no strangers to the silver screen.

Of course, Elvis had been a pretty big movie star himself. He made movies at first to stay in touch with his fans because he wasn't touring. But when it became clear how much the camera loved him—and what those close-up shots did to his female fans—the King made more films, *Blue Hawaii, Jailhouse Rock, Viva Las Vegas*, and *Love Me Tender*, to name just a few.

Colonel Parker thought George Strait had the looks, the charm, and the talent to make it big in movies. He felt George had the kind of charisma Elvis had, but Strait himself was skeptical. "Ninety percent of the time when an actor tries to become a singer or a singer tries to become an actor, it really doesn't work," he said. "But with the right people I think we can make a quality movie."

Parker wouldn't give up. "He just kept tellin' me, 'George, you gotta do movies.' " Strait says. "I didn't want country music people to look like hillbilly hicks, because they're not. And I wanted to sing in the movie and to do a soundtrack. I like rodeo, so we talked about putting rodeo scenes in there."

Woolsey liked the idea of a movie but, like Strait, he was understandably cautious. What would it mean to Strait's career? Would his fans fear he was abandoning country music for an acting career? Though everything he'd done to date had been successful, making a movie was a huge risk. As Strait himself put it, a George Strait movie might turn out to be "the worst thing you've ever seen."

Meanwhile, Colonel Parker introduced George Strait to Jerry Weintraub, who had produced the Robert Altman film *Nashville*, among others. Weintraub attended a few George Strait concerts and agreed that the camera would love him and that he could be a film star.

Strait agreed to consider a movie but wanted to see the script before committing himself. Soon they were looking at a script by Rex McGee, a Texas-born screenwriter with twenty years in the movie business.

In 1957, Elvis had starred in a movie called *Loving You*, in which he played a fast-rising rock-and-roll star named Deke Rivers, a nice guy who is tired of his big career. His manager is an older woman for whom he is just a commodity, not a person but an "act." One day he just up and leaves to return to his Texas roots.

The movie script presented to George Strait resembled the Elvis film in many ways. Its hero was a country star named Dusty Chandler who is tired of all the smoke and lights onstage. His manager, like the manager in *Loving You*, is an older woman (she would be played by Lesley Ann Warren). When Dusty walks off the stage to go back to his barroom roots, he falls in love with a young woman (Isabel Glasser) who lives on a ranch with her father and brothers.

The move was called *Pure Country*.

Strait's experience in the entertainment world was confined to live concerts and record albums. With twelve albums (not including three greatest hits collections) and countless hit singles, he had only released four promotional videos: "Amarillo by Morning," "The Chair," "Baby's Gotten Good at Goodbye," and "If I Know Me."

Even if he'd had more experience in video, making a full-length movie was still a whole other story. Not even his comfort in the recording studio could help prepare him for this.

In order to help Strait become comfortable in front of the camera, director Chris Cain made the decision to do the concert scenes first. These were filmed on May 7, 1992, at the Las Vegas Convention Center. Some lucky members of the George Strait fan club were in the audience.

The strategy worked. Strait said, "I was nervous going into it, but after the first scene, I kind of calmed down."

The concerts in the movie are filled with smoke and lights and lots of big rock-show elements that you'd never find at a real George Strait concert. In fact, that's one of the reasons the character Dusty is getting tired of life on the road. Nothing is real to him anymore.

As he looks out at the audience, Dusty begins to grow dizzy from all the craziness around him. In fact he deliberately sings off-key to prove to himself that the audience isn't even listening anymore. After the show his bodyguard and road manager are walking him off the stage, trying to hold back the fans who are clamoring to touch him. Dusty knows he hasn't done a good show. But his guys keep telling him how great it was, praising him in a way Dusty knows is empty and false.

Danny O'Brien, Strait's tour coordinator, who was once part of the band, has addressed this subject insofar as the real George Strait is concerned. "I think the hardest part of all this for George is not that he's any different than he ever was, but that all the rest of us are. . . . Even I look at him a little differently than I used to. When I first met him, he was just another hillbilly singer . . . but now, he's '*George Strait.*' "

Like the fans in the Las Vegas Convention Center, George Strait's fans who saw him in *Pure Country* gasped when he first appeared on the big screen. Dressed in extra-tight jeans and a white leather sequined jacket, he had a swagger to his walk and an attitude in his talk that was very different from the real George. He also had longer hair and a ponytail. He wasn't allowed to shave for about seven days of shooting in order to get that stubble that added to his look.

Later, Strait told CBS-TV's Mark McEwen something that had happened while he was sporting his beard. "We were eating one night and the waitress says, 'You know, you look just like George Strait.' I said, 'Oh really?' She said, 'Yeah, you do.' I said, 'Well, I'm a little better looking than he is, though, don't you think?' "

Filming a scene with actress Lesley Ann Warren, Strait said, "I was nervous as a cat and so was everybody else. Once I had rehearsed it a couple of times, she got really intense and made it real for me. She just told me to relax and try to be real, to listen to what she said and respond."

Moviemaking is a "little harder" than singing, Strait said. "But it's hard for me to remember how hard it was to walk on the stage for the first time."

In the film, Dusty makes his decision to walk away and shaves off the beard and cuts off the ponytail. He returns to the small Texas town of his youth and goes to see his grandma, who still has his old acoustic guitar. He visits a honky tonk where he gets into a fight defending the honor of a beautiful woman. As it turns out, she and her family need more of Dusty's help—to save their family ranch from the bill collectors. Dusty and the young woman decide to work together, competing in a rodeo for cash. And of course they fall in love.

"I felt like this was a movie that might not be all that hard for me for a first-time deal," Strait said. "I'm familiar with the concert stuff, I'm familiar with the rodeo stuff."

What made the movie even more fun for George Strait was the opportunity it gave him to do some real rodeo roping and riding. Of course, the Hollywood people were very nervous about his insistence that he do his own stunts. They went out to Texas, George's home ground, and shot not only the rodeo and riding scenes, but also some stunning shots of the beautiful Texas flatlands. Other scenes in Texas were filmed in Fort Worth and Waxahatchie.

Strait said he could understand Dusty's feeling of disillusionment and burnout in the movie. Mark McEwen asked him, "How much of that story is you up there onstage?"

"Well," Strait replied, "I can't relate to it to the extent that he does, where he just walks away from it. But when you go out and do two-thirty, two-forty dates a year, you know, come October, November, you're kind of feeling a little burned out and ready to quit. There were times when I thought, 'I can't do this another year.' So, you know, this guy just walks away from it, and finds other things that he remembers that he used to like to do that got him to where he was."

A movie about music starring one of the country music giants of the nineties obviously needed a sensational soundtrack. At the same time, George Strait now found himself with a new producer.

Tony Brown had been a keyboard player with Elvis and had produced albums for Steve Earle, the Mavericks, and Lyle Lovett. After Jimmy Bowen's departure, he become president of MCA Nashville. He was already a huge fan of Strait's.

"When he walks in a room—I mean, people like Johnny Cash have a presence," Brown told *The Journal of Country Music*. "People like Lyle Lovett have a presence. . . . George is about the fact that he's the real deal. He's a country superstar. He's a cowboy. He is a very cool-looking individual."

As an executive with MCA Records during the time Jimmy Bowen had been producing George Strait, Brown had observed Strait's technique in the studio. "[He] does what he does and the band falls into it," Brown said. "They don't play the same kind of licks they play on everybody else's records."

When Brown found out that he would be co-producing the *Pure Country* soundtrack with George Strait, there were only six weeks to prepare. A few songs had been written in advance. One was "Heartland," which turned out to be a huge number-one hit. At first it had the title "Pure Country" and lyrics that George and Tony Brown didn't like. The songwriters kept reworking it, changed the title, and it flew.

The music in the movie had to be a lot more electric and rocklike than the usual George Strait fare. "Heartland," the song whose lyrics celebrate twin fiddles and steel guitars, is filled with drums and electric guitars. "I had to remember this was not me—George Strait—doing an album," Strait said. "This was for the character in the movie to sing in a situation that wasn't real. Once I got past that, we cut it."

A touching moment for the star and everyone associated with *Pure Country* occurred when it was decided to use his son, Bubba, to sing the first few bars of "Heartland." Strait sat with him in the vocal booth to help him feel comfortable. The final soundtrack contains two versions of "Heartland." The one at the beginning is all rock and roll, and the one at the end is, well, pure country: stark, simple drum, fiddle, and steel and acoustic guitar.

"When Did You Stop Loving Me?" by Monty Holmes and Donny Kees became a number-six hit. "And I Cross My Heart," written by Steve Dorff and Eric Kaz, is the song at the end of the film that doesn't leave a dry eye in the house. It went to number one, and remains one of the songs that gets the biggest cheer at a George Strait concert.

Two songs by Jim Lauderdale appear on the soundtrack, "The King of Broken Hearts" and "Where the Sidewalk Ends." Tony Brown had been excited about pitching them to Strait. "I'm a Lauderdale fanatic," he says. "I love his songs and so I kept going, 'If we don't have anything else, I'm gonna go pitch these. These would be great. I bet George would love these.'

"Well, I played 'em for George at the studio and he went crazy. He said, 'Let's do these today.' And that's what we did. . . . The morning he heard 'em, he cut 'em that afternoon."

Jim Lauderdale says, "I found out about it just a couple of days later and I just couldn't believe the good news." It turns out that an A&R person at MCA Records had pitched those very two songs earlier to the movie people, who had passed on them.

Producer Jerry Weintraub believed George had a future as an actor. "The women are going to go nuts over this guy," he said. "The guys like him because he's a man's man. . . . And he's a great guy on top of everything else. I've enjoyed this experience with him more than anything else I've done in years."

Even Strait was happy with the outcome. "I don't see this as a risk," he said. "I see it as a new adventure. It's a real good change of pace for me to come out and try something new in the entertainment field. I'm glad I did it. The album turned out great. It's the first album I've ever done with Tony Brown and I enjoyed working with him. I hope we get to do a lot more together."

The weather was pure autumn on Wednesday, October 21, 1992. Outside the Dominion Country Club in San Antonio a stream of stretch limos dropped off their passengers, many wearing cowboy hats and spit-shined boots. A big party was taking place to celebrate the screening of *Pure Country* at the Northwest Theater.

Strait didn't stop smiling all night, and Norma was beaming. Earlier, he had told an interviewer, "Well, it is awfully nice to be in a movie. I know the real reason that I'm in this movie is because of my success in the music business. But, yeah, I guess everybody has dreams of being in a movie at one time or another. And I'm no exception.

"So I guess you could say—yeah, it is, like a dream come true."

Strait wore a black cowboy hat, bright blue shirt, tweed blazer, boots, and a big silver belt buckle engraved with his name. Producer Jerry Weintraub, director Christopher Cain, and actresses Isabel Glasser and Lesley Ann Warren were all a part of the crowd of about three hundred well-wishers. They dined on Texas barbecue and a Tex-Mex buffet elegantly served in silver chafing dishes.

When *Pure Country* premiered in Nashville, the audience included Garth Brooks, Randy Travis, Kathy Mattea, Lorrie Morgan, Mark Collie, and Joe Diffie. All of Strait's Nashville team from Erv Woolsey's office and MCA Records were there to witness an event that is rare in Nashville—a movie-premiere party.

One of the happiest people in the audience was songwriter Jim Lauderdale. "I was surprised when I saw the final cut of the movie," he said. "I knew they were going to use 'When the Sidewalk Ends' as part of George's character's last set, but they kept playing it over and over again. It was just such a huge thrill to be sitting there hearing my song coming from the movie screen. It was just a wonderful feeling."

Pure Country opened on October 23, 1992, and scored number six in *Variety*'s top box-office chart.

It grossed twenty million at the box office, according to Erv Woolsey, and has sold a million videos.

ACCLAIM FOR *PURE COUNTRY*

Winner of the Tex Ritter Award in 1992
from the Academy of Country Music

"*Pure Country* follows in a hallowed tradition: the '30s and '40s singing cowboy films of Gene Autry, Tex Ritter and Roy Rogers ... as for the music, there are some fine songs."
>   —Richard Harrington,
>   *The Washington Post*

"A genuine movie star is born—George Strait."
—Jimmy Carter, *Crook and Chase*, TNN

"*Pure Country* is a pure delight. A wonderful family film."
>   —Jim Ferguson, KMSB-TV, Tucson

"*Pure Country* is pure gold."
>   —Brian Linehan, CFRB Radio

"I was glad to see somebody finally did a country music film right. The bars, they look just like the ones at home . . . as far as [George Strait] as an actor, he has some real natural moments in there. I was happy to see it."

—Garth Brooks

"I enjoyed the film. The camera likes George; he looks great on film . . . as a singer sitting in the audience, there were a lot of things in this movie I could actually relate to."

—Randy Travis

"The movie did great things for my career," Strait says. "There's no question about it."

Pure Country brought George Strait a lot of new fans, many of them younger than those who'd previously been in his audiences. More than that, it was a positive experience for him.

"I really enjoyed doing the movie, and although I don't know that I could be a great actor, I do think I could make some movies," Strait said. "It's just something that came pretty easy, and although I didn't have to stretch a lot, I did do some things that were out of the ordinary for me and didn't really seem that hard."

The movie's soundtrack had been put together quickly, on instinct and the combined experience of George Strait and Tony Brown.

"It's amazing this album came out the way it did," Strait says.

Amazing indeed. The soundtrack has sold five million copies. It is the best-selling album of George Strait's career.

As for Strait's new producer, the experience of making that soundtrack was a great way to begin the relationship that has lasted to this day. "I think what I discovered on *Pure Country* was how talented George really is," Brown says, adding, "If he was a superstar before that, he became a bigger superstar after."

Will George Strait ever do another movie?

"If I do another one, I want to see if I can do something else," he said. "To do a *Pure Country II* would not be much of a challenge because I've already done that. I'd rather do a Western. Maybe there's an opportunity for that."

Hint to producers and directors: George Strait was asked to name his favorite movies and actors. He called Jack Nicholson "maybe the greatest actor of the decade" and said he loved him and Marlon Brando in *Missouri Breaks*. "*The Outlaw Josie Wales*, with Clint Eastwood, is probably my all-time favorite movie," he said.

At the Houston Livestock Show and Rodeo in March of 1993, two fans were eagerly waiting for George Strait and the Ace in the Hole Band to come onstage and play. The rest of the crowd was just as excited.

Suddenly these fans were approached by two men who told them they had to move out of their good seats. The two men were Secret Service agents assigned to guard former president George Bush, who had come to see George Strait at the show.

The fans were given two seats elsewhere and received an extra bonus for their trouble: after the show, they were taken backstage to meet George Strait.

"We thought it was kind of funny," one of them said.

In April 1993, the Academy of Country Music was given three solid hours on NBC for its twenty-eighth annual awards show. Hosted by George Strait, Reba McEntire, and Alabama's Randy Owen, this was the first country awards show to be given a whole night of network prime time. That it happened in the May sweeps month, when networks want the highest possible ratings so they can charge higher ad rates in the future, said something about the growing national popularity of country music. Six thousand people crowded into the amphitheater for the event and millions more watched at home.

ACM producer/director Gene Weed said, "This time around, country music's popularity is no *Urban Cowboy* flurry like it was in the seventies. This started when George Strait and Alabama broke out some years ago and it has never let up.

It gets bigger every year. But the biggest difference is, country music never had a young audience before and now it does, right down to the teens and subteens. Everybody loves it."

After being thrown together to produce the *Pure Country* soundtrack album in six short weeks, Tony Brown and George Strait soon had the opportunity to collaborate again, but this time in a less hurried fashion. Strait says, "I like Tony as a friend, I respect him as a producer, I respect him as a musician."

"He's a quick study," Tony Brown says of George Strait. "He comes to do work 'cause he wants to record his album, then he wants to get back to Texas."

Released in September of 1993, *Easy Come, Easy Go* had little to do with the hot young country music the movie and soundtrack had been about. Even after that big success, George Strait was still keeping it traditional. He chose Buck Owens–inspired tunes, tunes that were the heart of country in the 1960s in much the same way George Strait was in the eighties.

What could be more old-fashioned country than the song "Lovebug," written by Curtis Wayne and Wayne Kemp, which George Jones had made famous? Strait's twenty-fifth number-one single, the title track, "Easy Come, Easy Go," was written by Aaron Barker and Dean Dillon. Its Mexican-flavored sound is terrific music to his listeners' ears.

"The Man in Love with You," by Steve Dorff and Gary Harju, and "I'd Like to Have That One Back," written by Bill Shore, Rick West, and Aaron Barker, were both top-ten hits as well. "Without Me Around," written by Dean Dillon and John Northrup, is notable for its use of strings. Even when he's keepin' it country, George Strait occasionally indulges in some pop-inspired orchestrations.

Strait joined Ray Benson and an all-star cast for another landmark album in April of 1993. *Asleep at the Wheel Tribute to the Music of Bob Wills and the Texas Playboys* was a labor of love for Ray Benson. In addition to Strait, Benson included Chet Atkins, Suzy Bogguss, Garth Brooks, Brooks & Dunn, Vince Gill, Johnny Gimble, Merle Haggard, Huey Lewis, Lyle Lovett, Willie Nelson, Jody Nix, Lucky Oceans, Dolly Parton, Leon Rausch, Herb Remington, Riders in the Sky, Johnny Rodriguez, Eldon Shamblin, and Marty Stuart.

The album contains a dynamite duet of Strait and Ray Benson on the Bob Wills classic "Big Ball's in Cowtown." This is one of the few records that Strait recorded in a Texas studio, Bismeaux Studios in Austin.

"Asleep at the Wheel is a great group," he said, "and I know most of the guys in the band personally. I admire what they have done and have a lot of respect for the kind of music they do. We opened up for them at Gruene Hall. That's the place where Ray Benson is right in his element."

In the summer of 1994, George Strait and the Ace in the Hole Band played the Summit in Houston. He'd been playing there for years and was a prominent member of the Summit's Wall of Fame. He was in the company of other stars like Bruce Springsteen, Van Halen, ZZ Top, Willie Nelson, Prince, and Aerosmith—all of whose box-office receipts at the venue exceeded $1 million.

As they did every year, Strait and the band played to a sold-out house, providing their usual consistent low-key, high-quality show. They performed on a stage set up in the round, in the middle of the floor, with the band arranged in a circle. Strait moved among four microphones set up at each side of the stage. They did twenty-three songs, nearly half from *Pure Country* and *Easy Come, Easy Go*. As always, they sang some Bob Wills tunes, including "That's What I Like About the South" and "Milkcow Blues."

In 1994, the Ace in the Hole Band did something unusual for a touring band: they released their own first album, on Texas World Records. It's a good thing for the band to have their own career, separate from that of George Strait. When Strait isn't touring, the band does a lot of shows on their own.

November 1994 saw the release of the album *Lead On*, which debuted on the charts at number one. In his review, Mario Tarradell, critic for *The Dallas Morning News*, singled out "I Met a Friend of Yours Today," written by Wayland Holyfield and Bob McDill, for its new twist on country's usual cheatin' theme, but the big hit was "You Can't Make a Heart Love Somebody," about a man proposing to a woman who would love to be in love with him but, sadly, isn't. Written by Steve Clark and Johnny MacRae, it was Strait's forty-seventh charted single and his twenty-seventh *Billboard* number one. *Lead On* also boasted a song written by Nashville radio personalities Gerry House and Devon O'Day. "The Big One" became a number-one single.

Los Angeles Times reviewer Randy Lewis called *Lead On* "the best album of the Texan's long career. The songs ring true throughout . . . and the plentiful lyric twists always are in service of real emotion. His ballad singing takes a giant leap forward, displaying the nuanced inflection that separates the pros from the amateurs."

"George Strait is the Frank Sinatra of his era," Jimmy Bowen has claimed, and he ought to know. He's worked with both of them.

One evening during a stint in Texas, Sinatra actually invited Strait backstage right before the start of his show. "You just can't beat the big-band swing," Strait said. "He's such a great singer . . . he's a classy guy."

The big-band swing of Sinatra and the Western swing of Bob Wills, Asleep at the Wheel, and

George Strait have a lot in common. If you listen closely, you'll notice that some of Sinatra's songs, "One for My Baby," for example, have a kind of barroom sound. Songwriter Frank Dycus calls such music "urban honky tonk."

The Strait–Sinatra connection continued when another legendary record producer, Phil Ramone, asked Strait to sing on one of Sinatra's *Duets* albums. That album and a second, *Duets II*, were created in a unique manner. Through special fiber-optic phone lines, Sinatra and each of his various collaborators sang together from different studios.

Strait sang "Fly Me to the Moon" with Frank. He was thrilled by the opportunity to record with Frank Sinatra . . . even long-distance.

Where do you go when you're already at the top and have been there for more than a decade? Well, perhaps that's the best time for a look back.

CHAPTER SIX

Top of the Top

"I said from the very beginning that I wanted to have some longevity in this business," George Strait has stated, "and to be able to be around for a long time like Merle Haggard and George Jones and people like that." By 1995, that dream had become a reality.

Making one major album a year is enough for most artists, and George is no exception. Although he had scaled back his touring to seventy-five shows a year, he played in such big arenas that most of his fans still got a chance to see him. In the past few years, though, he'd done even fewer shows. "I love performing," he explained. "It's the going to and from concerts that's rough. It's not that I don't enjoy doing the shows, it's the time in between that you spend on the road and in the hotel rooms." When he first scaled back on touring he said, "I'm sure I'm leaving a lot of money out there on the table by doing that, but it's more important to me to be able to be happy and enjoy this rather than go out there and kill myself just for the money."

This is the new face of the American dream. Work is one part of life but there are other parts that are of equal or greater importance. "I have my own life—my other life when I'm off—that I choose to live," Strait told Jack Hurst of the *Austin American-Statesman*, "and I have my friends there that don't have anything to do with the music business. It's fun doing everything I can do with my son, because he's into a lot of things. And I play a lot of golf, and I hunt and fish, and I still rope. . . . I'm real fortunate right now to have the time to do the things that I really want to do and enjoy myself."

Strait makes no secret of the fact that he loves being at home in San Antonio or down on his ranch between San Antonio and Laredo, where the land is beautiful and the air is clear and sweet. "Some people," he's said, "live the music business from the time they wake up to the time they go to bed every day of their lives. I'm just not the kind of person who can do that."

We all have our own fantasy of a life of luxury and comfort and our own dream of what we would do if we ever became rich enough to do whatever we want to do. "I'd really like to have more time to concentrate on my team roping," Strait says.

George Strait knows what he wants. To run his ranch south of San Antonio. Ride his horses. Rope his cattle. Spend time with family and friends who have nothing to do with the music business. If he's "keepin' it country" in his music, in his life he is "keepin' it real."

"Hi! I'm John Strait. My son was born in Poteet, Texas, and grew up in Pearsall, Texas. He started singing when he was sixteen years old. He started singing old rock-and-roll songs but fell in love with country music around the time Merle Haggard recorded 'Okie from Muskogee.' His name is George Strait."

At the thirtieth annual Academy of Country Music Awards, televised on Wednesday, May 10, 1995, on NBC, a parent of each of the nominees for Top Male and Top Female Vocalist of the Year introduced his or her child.

This made front-page news in the *Frio-Nueces Current*, published in Pearsall, Frio County, Texas. The newspaper boasts, "Now in our 100th year! Largest Circulation Weekly Between San Antonio and Laredo." A reporter from the paper filed the story from Nashville with the headline STRAIT INTRODUCES SON AT AWARDS SHOW.

Strait's competitors for Top Male Vocalist were Vince Gill, Alan Jackson, Garth Brooks, and Joe Diffie. Though he didn't win—the award went to Alan Jackson—it had to be a thrill for the Straits to participate together in the nationally televised show.

Strait told an interviewer he'd "been fortunate to have things happen in my career at times when they needed to happen—whether it's been

changing producers and having a little more free-
dom in the material—or a movie comes along
when doing a movie would certainly do a lot of
things for my career."

MCA Records' suggestion to George Strait that
he do a boxed set, a retrospective of his career to
date, was another such occurrence. "It didn't
take much arm twisting to me," Strait says. "I
just think it was a neat thing. You see a lot of
boxed sets, and usually the people you see them
on aren't here anymore. So I was happy to be
able to do one now while things are still looking
great for me."

As he had done for all his albums since *Does
Fort Worth Ever Cross Your Mind*, Strait put himself in charge of every aspect of the boxed set.
When *Strait Out of the Box* was released in September of 1995, it was obvious that George Strait
had found doing it a labor of love.

The first task was to select the songs.

Since 1981, George Strait had released nine-
teen albums, containing a total of one hundred
and ninety songs. He had recorded numerous
other songs as well, but for one reason or another, these had not been released.

Then there were the eight songs that he and the
Ace in the Hole Band had recorded in the mid-
1970s for Big D Records in Houston. Over the
years, Strait's fans have come to know and admire his ability to choose superb songs, but most

were probably unaware of the fact that he had written some of his own early in his career.

So it was that the three songs that open the first disk of the four-disk set are George Strait's own compositions, taken from those original Big D sessions. "I Just Can't Go On Dying Like This," "(That Don't Change) The Way I Feel About You," and "I Don't Want to Talk It Over Anymore" are exciting to listen to. They are our only opportunity to hear the voice we have come to love over the years in its earliest recorded form. Like seeing early paintings by a famous artist or the first movie appearances of stars we've grown with over the years, the experience of hearing these three songs takes us back to the roots of the giant talent we admire today.

In the booklet that accompanies the package, Strait talks about the three Big D songs to journalist Kay West. "I wrote these songs and you might be able to hear, when you listen to [them], why my songwriting didn't develop the way I wanted it to. They're not bad songs but you can see what a rookie I was, just a young guy trying to get started in country music. A foolish kid who didn't know any better."

Strait Out of the Box contains some other previously unreleased songs as well, including "What Would Your Memories Do?" by Hank Cochran and Dean Dillon, and Lee Emerson's "I Thought I Heard You Calling My Name." Strait hadn't forgotten that he'd liked these tunes, and the boxed set was a great chance to share them with his audience.

Probably the most exciting previously unreleased tune in *Strait Out of the Box* is his duet with Frank Sinatra. George Strait had been disappointed that his duet with Sinatra, the Bart Howard composition "Fly Me to the Moon," had not appeared on the albums. What a treat for fans to hear today's most beloved singing cowboy join forces with the Chairman of the Board on such a wonderful and classic tune.

All of Strait's number-one hits join other classics from his albums, *Holding My Own* being the album from which the most selections were included. These were included because that album had not received the attention it deserved, coming out as it did in the same year as *Pure Country*. "Trains Make Me Lonesome" by Paul Overstreet and Thom Schuyler, "So Much Like My Dad" by Chips Moman and Bobby Emmons, "Wonderland of Love" by Curtis Wayne, and "Gone As a Girl Can Get" by Jerry Max Lane are songs that could easily have reached number one had they been issued as singles at another time.

Summing it all up, Strait said, "Some of the songs I cut I'm really proud of. I didn't write them. I just cut them. I still think they were great songs." And it's true: everything about *Strait Out of the Box* is first-class, from the box featuring a photograph of real branded leather to the booklet to the inserts in each of the four CDs. For fans who were late in discovering George Strait, it offered a complete musical history of an artist everyone recognized as pivotal to the history of country music in the 1980s and 1990s.

It was a great trip down memory lane. "You go back and you start remembering what led up to this song, why you picked it, where you heard it," Strait said. "It was fun to remember all that. I enjoyed making it. I gotta be pushed into a lot of things, but I was glad about this one. . . . Remembering some of the old clubs that we played, and loading and unloading equipment in the back of our truck . . . seeing how things progressed was real interesting for me," he said.

A bonus for fans who bought the set was the inclusion of two brand-new songs. "I Know She Still Loves Me," written by Aaron Barker and Monty Holmes, was a great new cut and another radio hit. "Check Yes or No" by Danny M. Wells and Dana Hunt Oglesby reached number one on the *Billboard* chart and stayed there for four weeks. It became an instant favorite among Strait's legions of fans. It also brought him many new ones, who related to the song's story of a note being passed in a classroom between a boy and girl who have crushes on each other.

Strait Out of the Box has outsold every boxed set in country music history. That's amazing enough. Even more so is the fact that it is tied for second place in best-selling boxed sets of all time *in all forms of music*. It shares that spot with Led Zeppelin's retrospective and is surpassed only by Bruce Springsteen's.

Even the man himself was impressed. "Its success really did surprise me," Strait says. "We did have a lot of help though, because 'Check Yes or No' was such a big record, and the boxed set was really the only place to find it."

This huge success was further proof that fans were "voting with their pocketbook." "To be able to take fifteen years and compile it in one boxed set as a finished product and be something I could be really proud of is a great feeling for me," Strait said. "It came at a good time in my career. Hopefully, I'll be around for fifteen more years to put out another one."

Needless to say, his fans hope so, too.

When the Country Music Association Awards nominations were announced in August of 1995, George Strait was nominated for Male Vocalist of the Year, but for the first time in a long while he was not nominated for Entertainer of the Year. Strait said he "doesn't lose any sleep over it," but also said it "hurts not to get nominated in Entertainer of the Year."

"I'm still just as competitive as I ever was in that respect," he says about awards. "I mean, it's not really like I'm competing with the other artists out there. I don't look at it that way, but I'm really kind of competing with myself. I always want to do better and better. So that is kind of an acknowledgment, when you get an award, that you've done well. I still love to win and I still love to have number-one records. And I always will."

In the fall of 1995, Strait was honored with ASCAP's Voice of Music Award for his "interpretations of great songs, which have touched the hearts and minds of music lovers throughout the world."

After the huge success of the boxed set, expectations were high for his next album. Record retailers who had been thrilled with the sales of *Strait Out of the Box* felt that the singer was poised for the biggest record of his career. And along with those expectations came the pressure a performer feels to outdo his previous successes. "My expectations are always up," Strait says. "I feel pressure every time I go into the studio to do an album. Every artist is that way; they want to do something better than they've ever done before."

In the end, pressure or no pressure, the retailers weren't disappointed. In April of 1996, *Blue Clear Sky* offered its first single, the title track. The song instantly hit number one.

Once again it was a case of a last-minute decision. " 'Blue Clear Sky' showed up the morning of the last day we were recording that album," Tony Brown said. "When it came in [George] loved it, and it took him about thirty minutes to learn. Then he went in the studio and recorded it."

"I know it when it hits me," Strait says. But when he first heard "Blue Clear Sky," he was concerned about the lyrics. "I thought that 'Blue Clear Sky' didn't sound right to me, it should

have been 'Clear Blue Sky,' " he said. "We talked
about it, and we came close to messing it up. We
finally called Bob DiPiero [one of the song's writ-
ers] and he said he got the line from *Forrest
Gump*. So it all made sense to me." Two more hit
singles from *Blue Clear Sky* were "I Can Still
Make Cheyenne," written by Aaron Barker and
manager Erv Woolsey, and "Carried Away," written
by Steve Bogard and Jeff Stevens.

The *Houston Chronicle* said *Blue Clear Sky* was
"not only Strait's deepest effort in several years,
it was arguably the best mainstream country album to come out of Nashville last year."

New Country's review of the album cited George
Strait's great song-picking skills and ear for
melody, calling his vocals "detailed works of
beauty." Reviewer Robert Baird said, "*Blue Clear
Sky* is simply Strait doing Strait, which is another
way of saying that hat acts have come and gone,
but George Strait has outlasted them all."

The album has already been certified platinum.

On September 25, the Country Music Hall of
Fame and Museum, which sits atop music row at
the corner of Music Square East and Division
Street, was the site of a very special party.

Actually, every day is a celebration in this Music City landmark that calls itself the Cornerstone
of Country and is run by the Country Music Foundation. Inside the Hall of Fame, impressive brass
plaques commemorate the giants of country music, those still with us and those who have passed

on. Elvis's gold piano and Webb Pierce's Silver
Dollar Bonneville sit alongside great costumes,
old guitars, and original sheet music, all the richly
evocative artifacts of the great country music
tradition.

On this particular evening, MCA Records was
holding a reception to show its appreciation for
George Strait's fifteen years of number-one hits
and almost forty million records sold. All of the
executives and staff who work behind the scenes
at MCA and at Erv Woolsey Management were on
hand. As a special gift for the occasion, MCA gave
George a fourteen-week-old Australian cattle dog,
commonly called a "Blueheeler," that had been
flown in from Australia.

Bruce Hinton, chairman of MCA Nashville, welcomed the guests and presented Strait with a triple-
platinum plaque symbolizing sales of three million
copies of *Strait Out of the Box*. MCA Nashville
president Tony Brown, Strait's coproducer, gave
him a quintuple-platinum plaque for *Pure Country*. As if that wasn't enough stuff to carry back
home to Texas, Strait was also presented with
triple-platinum plaques for *Greatest Hits Volume
One* and *Greatest Hits Volume Two* and a double-
platinum plaque for *Ocean Front Property*.

To cap off the excitement, George Strait do-
nated a *Pure Country* poster, script, jacket, and hat
to the Country Music Foundation, as well as the
original branded leather that had been photo-
graphed for the cover of the boxed set, and the
boxed set itself.

Last but not least, he gave the foundation a George Strait Resistol hat.

Blue Clear Sky was the Country Music Association's pick for Album of the Year at its 1996 awards show. George Strait was named Male Vocalist of the Year. And "Check Yes or No" was named Single of the Year.

"It's been a while since I walked up these stairs," Strait said as he went up to accept one of the evening's three awards. "I want to thank my dad for his support. Now he's sitting down there in Pearsall, Texas, watching us," he continued. "Thank you, Daddy."

Later, he beamed as he told reporters, "As long as they want to give them to me, I'll keep taking them."

MCA Nashville chairman Bruce Hinton said, "I look at George Strait as being as hot as he's ever been in his career. The new single is the highest debuting single for George in eight years.

"Everyone talks about hat acts," Hinton continued, "but they sometimes forget that he's the original hat act. He's the one who started it all. To be in this business for fifteen years and be as hot as he is now is a real testament to the quality of his music and also to the charisma he brings to his live performances."

At the nationally broadcast Academy of Country Music Awards show in April 1997, George Strait was awarded Top Male Vocalist of the Year.

And the Album of the Year honor was given to George Strait, Tony Brown, and MCA Records for *Blue Clear Sky*.

When his name was announced, George Strait received a full one-minute standing ovation.

"I'm almost embarrassed," he said.

Later, when he was asked to describe the key to his success, he grinned and said, "I'm not telling anybody."

Getting awards is something that matters even to modest stars like George Strait. "I've gone through some years when the awards haven't come, so for me to pick up another one is real exciting," he says. "It's still an honor to be nominated and know that people appreciate what you do."

Hot is hot. And then there's hotter.

On May 17, 1997, one day before his forty-fifth birthday, George Strait became only the sixth country artist in the 1990s to hit the top of the pop chart—the *Billboard* 200. It is the chart on which all musical styles compete against each other.

Billboard had published this list three hundred and ninety-nine times to date, and country artists had seen their names atop it for a total of only fifty-seven weeks. With Garth Brooks claiming eighteen of those weeks and Billy Ray Cyrus seventeen, there wasn't a whole lot of room left for anyone else. John Michael Montgomery, Tim McGraw, and LeAnn Rimes had also been honored with that top spot.

On May 17, George Strait's twenty-second album, *Carrying Your Love with Me*, hit number one on that important chart, beating out Mary J. Blige *(Share My World)* and the Spice Girls *(Spice)*.

"It's a very big deal for country music," Ed Benson, the executive director of the CMA, told *Country Weekly*. "It speaks well for country music to know that we have artists that can sell more product than any other artist in the country."

KEEPIN' COUNTRY ON TOP

Garth Brooks was the first of the 1990s country superstars to top the pop charts, but six others were there before he'd even recorded one hit.

BOBBIE GENTRY

The Mississippi native's mysterious song "Ode to Billie Joe" had people all over America talking—and drove the album of the same name to the top of the pop and country charts in October 1967.

JOHNNY CASH

He sang his big hit "A Boy Named Sue" to cheering prisoners. The live album of that historic event, *Johnny Cash at San Quentin*, helped along by his TV show, jumped to number one.

GLEN CAMPBELL

He and his music entered America's living rooms every week with *The Glen Campbell Goodtime Hour*. In 1968, viewers and fans made Glen's album *Wichita Lineman* number one.

ELVIS PRESLEY

Elvis's 1973 one-hour concert in Honolulu was seen by a billion people the world over. The soundtrack album, *Aloha from Hawaii via Satellite*, released worldwide, was a natural number-one pop hit.

JOHN DENVER

The CMA's 1975 Entertainer of the Year had five top-ten country hits and seven top-twenty pop tunes on two albums, *Back Home Again* and *Windsong*. Both albums hit number one on the pop charts.

KENNY ROGERS

He'd been a favorite among American listeners for years. After the appearance of his *Greatest*

Hits album at the top of the pop chart in 1980, there was a ten-year gap until Garth did it again.

George Strait was characteristically modest when he heard the news.

"Success is giving people what they want," he said, "and I feel I've been fortunate enough to give people what they want. It's that simple."

Coproducer Tony Brown, with plenty to be proud of himself, said, "He's making the best music he's ever made and he just keeps getting better. Everybody in country music is really fascinated by George Strait. He's proof of the longevity of an artist in country music if the artist is that good.

"George, I think you can safely say, has become an icon. There's not one doubt in anybody's mind that George is a traditional country artist. He's a real cowboy from Texas, and he's a traditional artist who's never really strayed far from what he does and doesn't intend to. He's a breath of fresh air and yet he's been around for a lot of years."

Strait echoed the feelings of many of his fans when he said, "It seems like I always say this, but I believe that this might be one of the best albums I've ever recorded."

The album's first number-one single was "One Night at a Time," written by Earl Bud Lee, Eddie

Kilgallon, and Roger Cook. It stayed in the number-one position for five weeks.

The title song, "Carrying Your Love with Me," written by Jeff Stevens and Steve Bogard, was an instant success as well. "It was the first song that I kept when I started listening to songs for the album," he said, "and so I was able to really live with this song for a long time. And sometimes when you do that, after a while they don't hold up, and you end up passing on them, but this one held up then, and it's still holding up for me. I love this song. The melody is really really good and the chorus is what grabs you."

The single was number one—again, for five weeks.

George Strait's video for "Carrying Your Love with Me" was directed by the man who directed the movie *Pure Country*, Chris Cain. Cain is also the father of TV's Superman, *Lois and Clark* star Dean Cain. If you look closely at the video, you'll see that it is Dean Cain who is driving a motorcycle in the video. There's a woman on the back of the motorcycle, a very attractive blonde who happens to be Norma Strait, George's wife. Just call it All in the Family!

USA Today gave *Carrying Your Love with Me* three and a half stars and cited Strait's "sheer effortlessness and perfect phrasing." *Entertainment Weekly* said what fans had known for years: "Strait is still country's top dog."

Strait says, "I feel the mixture of the material is pretty broad. From a song like 'The Nerve' to

'Won't You Come Home (And Talk to a Stranger)'
covers a lot of area, if you know what I mean."
"The Nerve" was written by Bobby Braddock, and
"Won't You Come Home (And Talk to a Stranger)"
was written by Wayne Kemp.

For each of his albums, Strait likes to reach
back into the past and remake a tune. In this
case, it was an old Vern Gosdin song, "Today My
World Slipped Away," written with Mark Wright.
The third single was released in the fall of '97
and, like its predecessors, began its climb up the
charts right away.

"George's music is honest," Brown says. "He
never tries to follow any trends happening in
country music. He just does what he does. He
genuinely loves it."

Carrying Your Love with Me was named by the
Country Music Association as Album of the Year.
It has already gone platinum. It spent weeks
at the top of *Billboard*'s country chart and entered the pop chart at number two before moving
into the top spot.

"I would have loved to have been a professional rodeo roper," George Strait has said on a
number of occasions, "but when it came time for
me to choose a career, Norma and I had just gotten married and country music seemed to have a
better future.

"Looking back, I guess that I made the right
decision, but rodeo will always be an important
part of my life. There are team-roping events put

on just for guys in their fifties and sixties, so I'll be able to do this for a long time."

Welcome to Kingsville, Texas, home of the annual George Strait Team Roping Classic and Concert.

You can see why George Strait loves it here. The temperature is balmy year-round and the land is spectacular. Located in the heart of south Texas, Kingsville's main attraction is the historic King Ranch, a National Historic Landmark that is recognized as the birthplace of the American ranching industry. Founded in 1853, King Ranch covers 825,000 acres where sixty thousand head of cattle and three hundred quarter horses roam. Visitors to the ranch can see the wildlife of south Texas and then spend some time exploring the city, where a variety of shops offer contemporary and historic items. Among the attractions on the campus of nearby Texas A&M University is the Connor Museum, dedicated to preserving the history of the land that straddles the United States and Mexico.

Outside of singing and his family, Strait says the rodeo is his true love. "I'd do most anything to be a permanent part of it," he says. One way of doing so is to sponsor his annual rodeo show. And there's no better place to do so than Kingsville, the real land of the American cowboy, where ranching and riding and roping, the ways of life that George Strait has always known, are what living is still all about. It's no wonder that this is the place he wants to spend his time.

George's brother, Buddy, helped him found the event in 1983. Norma and Buddy's wife, Denise, act as the event's organizers each year. During the roping classic, George Strait is not a star; he's just one of the crowd. "Our team-roping event is probably one of the best in the country," he says. "We get the best ropers, including many professional ropers who compete in the national finals in Las Vegas."

It's a great weekend full of events. On Thursday night a George Strait fan meeting takes place at Country Luau, a little county bar in Kingsville. Team roping starts at around nine o'clock on Friday morning and goes on until mid-afternoon. "I got hooked on roping when I was in college," Strait said. "Roping is like taking up golf. You have a good day and you want to go back for more."

When it comes time to take his turn, Strait wants to be regarded as just another one of the competitors. Still, it's a thrill for the audience to know they're watching *the* George Strait when he and his partner have their moment in the sun.

Team roping involves two riders on horseback. The "header" gets the head; the "heeler" gets the rear hooves. When the steer is let out of the chute, Strait and his partner—this year it was champion cowboy Brett Beach—are each waiting on either side of the steer on horses. George sends his loop out and snares the steer's horns, while Beach snags the hooves. "I find roping to be very difficult," Strait says. "But these guys make it look so easy."

Back in 1990, when he'd attended the Big Spring Cowboy Reunion Rodeo, he told an interviewer that while he was now accustomed to performing onstage, entering the rodeo was scary. "I'm already nervous going in there and the crowd makes it worse," he said. "The only way to get used to it is to go out there and do it."

He's been doing it ever since.

The United States Team Roping Championships is a nine-year-old organization with eighty thousand members. "George's event is big, big," says Scott Sharp, its spokesman. "It's getting bigger every year."

Indeed, two hundred and fourteen teams were registered to rope in the fifteenth annual classic. Tickets for the roping events were completely sold out. "The roster of the George Strait classic reads like a Who's Who in Team Roping," says the "Voice of Rodeo" arena announcer Pete Wright. "You've got the best of the best riding and roping here today."

On Friday night everyone enjoys some of the most lip-smackin' barbecue they'll ever taste. It costs twenty dollars for all you can eat and you get some gambling chips you can use to win team-roping classic merchandise.

The finals take place on Saturday. Winners of the roping competition receive cash and hand-crafted, engraved leather saddles. The 1997 grand prize was a four-door, five-speed Chevy 545 pickup truck with a Bruton trailer attached—one for each partner on the winning team.

Strait's son, George Jr., and Buddy's sons, Trey and Walker, are a big part of the event. "They've kind of grown up with this roping," Strait told *Country Weekly*. "This is our fifteenth year and they're fifteen and sixteen years old. It's just kind of come natural to them. They get to see all these great ropers here and the ropers have influenced them a lot. All the kids have come a long way.

"Every year they keep getting better and better. It's been real fun to see them improve. All three of our boys are rodeoing and I think that's what they want to do. So I tell them you've got to go to college and get on a rodeo team there. After you finish college, if you want to rodeo, get after it."

Saturday night is really exciting for fans of George Strait's music. That's when he puts on the big concert that is the grand finale of the whole event. The focus here is even more strongly on swing music than usual.

During the proceedings, Texas Governor George W. Bush sent his congratulations. "Texas can be proud that one of our own gives his name and talent to this event so that fans and ropers alike can enjoy great family entertainment," he said.

"I miss being able to go into the honky tonks and play dances," George Strait has said. "I really like it when people can get up and dance."

Those honky tonks are where it all began for George Strait—the little clubs on the side of the road where for a few bucks you can hear some great music, have a few drinks, and leave the cares of the day behind. The sawdust floors and ceiling fans and all the folks in between, dancing to the music you're making, is what it takes to make a musician happy.

To be a legend when you're only in your forties is a rare occurrence. To be known as the bridge between the past and the future of country music is an astonishing accomplishment and one that even the modest George Strait has to acknowledge is true.

GEORGE STRAIT'S NUMBER-ONE HITS: THE COMPLETE LIST

Here's a list of all of George Strait's number-one hit singles, the year they hit, and the songwriters who penned them.

"Fool Hearted Memory"
1982
Byron Hill, Alan R. Mevis

"Amarillo by Morning"
1983
Terry Stafford, Paul Fraser

"A Fire I Can't Put Out"
1983
Darryl Staedtler

"You Look so Good in Love"
1983
Rory Bourke, Glen Ballard, Kerry Chaer

"Right or Wrong"
1984
Arthur L. Sizemore, Haven Gillespie,
Paul Biese

"Let's Fall to Pieces Together"
1984
Dickey Lee, Tommy Rocco, Johnny Russell

"Does Fort Worth Ever Cross Your Mind"
1984
Sanger D. Shafer, Darlene Shafer

"The Chair"
1985
Hank Cochran, Dean Dillon

"Nobody in His Right Mind Would've Left Her"
1986
Dean Dillon

"It Ain't Cool to be Crazy About You"
1986
Dean Dillon, Royce Porter

"Ocean Front Property"
1986
Dean Dillon, Hank Cochran, Royce Porter

"All My Ex's Live in Texas"
1987
Sanger D. Shafer, Lyndia J. Shafer

"Am I Blue"
1987
David Chamberlain

"Famous Last Words of a Fool"
1988
Dean Dillon, Rex Houston

"Baby Blue"
1988
Aaron Barker

"If You Ain't Lovin' (You Ain't Livin')"
1988
Tommy Collins

"Baby's Gotten Good at Goodbye"
1988
Tony Martin, Troy Martin

"What's Going on in Your World?"
1989
David Chamberlain, Royce Porter

"Ace in the Hole"
1989
Dennis Adkins

"Love Without End, Amen"
1990
Aaron Barker

"I've Come to Expect It from You"
1990
Dean Dillon, Buddy Cannon

"If I Know Me"
1991
Dean Dillon, Pam Belford

"You Know Me Better Than That"
1991
Tony Haselden, Anna Lisa Graham

"The Chill of an Early Fall"
1991
Green Daniel, Gretchen Peters

"So Much Like My Dad"
1992
Chips Moman, Bobby Emmons

"I Cross My Heart"
1992
Steve Dorff, Eric Kaz

"Heartland"
1992
Steve Dorff, John Bettis

"When Did You Stop Loving Me?"
1993
Monty Holmes, Donny Kees

"Easy Come, Easy Go"
1993
Aaron Barker, Dean Dillon

"I'd Like to Have That One Back"
1993
Bill Shore, Rick West, Aaron Barker

"You Can't Make a Heart Love Somebody"
1994
Steve Clark, Johnny MacRae

"The Big One"
1995
Gerry House, Devon O'Day

"Lead On"
1995
Dean Dillon, Teddy Gentry

"Check Yes or No"
1995
Danny M. Wells, Dana Hunt Oglesby

"I Know She Still Loves Me"
1995
Aaron Barker, Monty Holmes

"Blue Clear Sky"
1996
Mark D. Sanders, John Jarrard, Bob DiPiero

"Carried Away"
1996
Steve Bogard, Jeff Stevens

"I Can Still Make Cheyenne"
1996
Aaron Barker, Erv Woolsey

"One Night at a Time"
1997
Earl Bud Lee, Eddie Kilgallon, Roger Cook

"Carrying Your Love with Me"
1997
Jeff Stevens, Steve Bogard

What other performer today can please fans of so many ages and musical tastes? If you love country, well, of course you love George Strait. But if you love the music of Bing Crosby and Perry Como, you can also find plenty of songs on the twenty-two albums of George Strait to keep you entertained all night.

If you admire some of the finest storytelling that can be found anywhere—the wonderful country songs created by the songwriters of the past five decades—George Strait has chosen some of the best ones for you. Like a sense of humor and whimsy in your music? Strait has plenty of that, too.

"I don't moonwalk or break-dance or do the alligator," Strait says, "but I've got a great band and I take a lot of pride in some of my songs. I think they affect people."

Country Music Association executive director Ed Benson echoes the assessment of many. "George Strait was a principal advocate of traditional country music and was a bellwether as far as affecting a major trend. Just as importantly, he has sustained a career over a long period in a way that I don't think we'll be seeing much anymore. There will be fewer artists making an industry impact in the way George Strait has. He has remained true to his standards and true to his music. He's grown but he hasn't changed and he has been very good for country music."

If George Strait came to Nashville today looking for a record deal, people might say, well, we already have a lot of acts doing traditional country, wearing hats and jeans. But he is the original, and the reason why all these young guys in their twenties and thirties are even here in the first place.

"It's getting so it's hard to keep track of them," Strait says, laughing. "It used to be that a new artist doing traditional music would come along only occasionally, but now it seems like it's happening every other month. But that's good for country music."

Strait's fans, and fans of every kind of music, would have missed out on a lot if Strait hadn't been given that first chance. But we can all be glad he's showing no signs of slowing down. At age forty-five, he takes good care of himself and looks terrific. He plays golf and enjoys skiing. All that riding and roping on his ranch keeps him trim, even though his favorite foods are reportedly chicken-fried steak and Spanish rice. And he's a man who knows who he is and what he wants to do. He always has.

"I know I'm going to keep doing it as long as I can," he says, "as long as people like it and keep coming out to the shows. . . . I've got no intentions of slowing down."

His performance on the big screen in *Pure Country* is still remembered well, and he's been offered more movie roles. But now he has his life paced just the way he wants it. By cutting down on the touring, he has gotten the time he wants to spend at home.

"Privacy is real important to me," he says, "to have another life besides the one that I have when I'm out on the road when I'm doing what I do as a country music singer or entertainer or whatever you want to call it.

"I don't always want to be the country music singer, especially when I'm at home."

One ambition he has is to be inducted into the Country Music Hall of Fame, where the bronze plaque honoring him will hang on the wall next to his heroes George Jones and Merle Haggard, Lefty Frizzell and Floyd Tillman, and, of course, Bob Wills. He'd probably like that to happen while he's still alive.

"Yeah, no one knows if you know you got it, when you get it after you're gone," he said.

George Strait is a real man making music that is real. There isn't a false note or contrived lyric in the songs he picks. They are timeless country songs that will keep George Strait very much in the memory of millions of people long into the future.

"I like to think talent had a lot to do with it," he says. "The material has been good and the timing had a lot to do with it. . . . I'm a country singer. I don't want to be in the middle of the road. A fella could get run over out there."

George Strait says people often tell him, "Well, you've accomplished all you can in country music." He answers, "I don't feel that way. I'm not through, and I think I've got a lot more to go."

What does he still want to do in his career?

"Well, I've never been one to make a lot of big plans," he says, "but I've just kind of gone along and done things, and fortunately they worked out. I've always said that I wanted to do a totally swing album, and of course it's been done before. Merle Haggard did the tribute to Bob Wills album, but I still like to listen to the big-band swing with the Sinatra-type stuff that I've added, a little bit, into some of my albums. I thought that the Natalie Cole album, the tribute to her dad, was really, really great, and I enjoyed that a lot. Maybe someday I'll do an album of old Sinatra-flavored swing with a big huge band."

As to the future of country music, "I just don't see it going back to leaning more toward a cross-over kind of record," he says. "I hear a lot of good country music out there today."

The man who has made a stellar career out of keepin' it country has a lot of faith in the music. "I think it's in a pretty healthy state," he says. "If you'll look at country music's history, it kind of has a way of taking care of itself and always seems to come back around to its roots."

Strait's fans can be sure he'll never abandon the hard-core traditional country he loves best.

"This is one guy who walks it like he talks it," said *The Dallas Morning News*. "He was country when country wasn't cool, and if it's not ever cool again, he'll still be country."

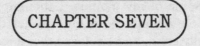

CHAPTER SEVEN

Keepin' It Country

You gotta love Texas. It is such a great place. Smart, friendly people. The slow, easy drawl of folks who love to tell a story. The vastness of the land and the glittering sophistication of the cities make the Lone Star State a great place to visit— and a great place to live.

San Antonio loves its hometown son George Strait. There's even talk from time to time of naming a street after him. The whole town gets excited over his Labor Day show at the Alamodome. In five short years, the George Strait Country Music Festival has turned into a major end-of-summer event and another great reason for tourists to visit the beautiful, lively, and colorful city. When television stations KENS-TV and KSAT-TV offered ticket giveaways for the fifth annual show, they were flooded with calls. It got so bad that callers were told all circuits were busy. Some people trying to connect to the Internet were unable to dial in during the 10:00 P.M. newscasts.

"It's special because it's at home," Strait says

about having the show in his hometown. "I want to work San Antonio, and the Alamodome is the perfect place to have something like that [show]."

The 1997 show was the last George Strait concert of the season, a season in which he broke his own attendance records even while playing only ten big shows. Not surprisingly, in light of this fact, a recent Harris Poll ranked George Strait among America's top-ten favorite singers.

"Some of my fans thought I was on the verge of retiring," he told *Country Weekly*. "But that's not true. It's just unbelievable to me that they're still coming out to the shows. It's so great to have fans like that."

Just three weeks before the Labor Day festival, Garth Brooks had put country music into the national spotlight in a big way. Country's megastar had attracted more than 250,000 fans to his free concert in New York's Central Park that was beamed by HBO into millions of homes.

Some New Yorkers were completely amazed that *country* music could be so big in a city better known for its operas, symphonies, and big rock shows. But their country cousins sure showed them a thing or two!

At the Central Park show, Garth Brooks, native son of Oklahoma, invited two of New York's greatest musical native sons, Billy Joel and Don McLean, to join him onstage.

With his three-hundred-and-sixty-foot stage, major smoke and lights, and incredibly rockin' stage show, Garth Brooks is almost the opposite of the laid-back George Strait and his very traditional singing style onstage. But as Garth has said time and again: "I am doing what I am doing today because of the Good Lord, my family, and George Strait."

One of country's newest stars has also made it clear that without George Strait today's country music scene would be far different. "By the time I got into high school," Lee Ann Womack said, "the *Right or Wrong* album was huge and he exposed lots of people to music they'd never heard. Everybody wanted to dress, talk, and walk like him. Everybody wanted to be him. He has done a tremendous job."

The singer of such new hits as "Never Again, Again" by Monty Holmes, who has written a number of hits for George Strait, and "The Fool," Lee Ann Womack was the first performer to take the stage at the fifth annual George Strait Country Music Festival.

You couldn't have asked for a prettier day. Saturday, August 30, dawned bright and blue, with balmy temperatures and relatively low humidity. A morning stroll along River Walk, the lush, tree-lined path that winds its way through downtown San Antonio along the San Antonio River, found dozens of people wearing George Strait T-shirts.

By noon, cars heading in the direction of the city's huge Alamodome filled East Commerce

Street, South St. Mary's Street, and the streets around the Alamo Plaza. George Strait bumper stickers were everywhere. On a black car someone had painted in big white letters WE LOVE GEORGE STRAIT. The sounds of George Strait songs were blasting from car radios and cassette players.

It's a Labor Day tradition for San Antonio radio stations to play everything Strait has ever recorded. One listener was the star himself. "I was playing golf and listening to the radio," he said, "listening to all this and I heard songs I had totally forgotten about. I really enjoyed that. . . . I started thinking, 'Man, I need to do that song again in my show!' I'm going to try and do that, to work some of them in. I used to do a lot of them. As time goes on, you drop one here, and you drop one there. You do new stuff."

Fans of all ages and ethnic groups lined up outside the Alamodome. Country cowboys, future farmers, computer programmers, retired senior citizens, young administrative assistants—they were all talking about how much they loved George Strait and which songs were their favorites.

"My audience is definitely changing," Strait said. "It used to be mostly older people coming to the show. Now I have young folks, too, that have to be into country music. And I mean young. Some of them aren't even in high school yet."

One young woman was carrying a huge poster that said CHECK YES OR NO with a big red check mark in the box next to YES. Two guys from Tyler,

Texas, were heard to remark that there are only three things in life besides work: girls, golf, and George Strait. A retired nurse from Dallas said she makes it her business to see Strait whenever and wherever he performs in Texas.

Women were wearing a variety of outfits, from plain jeans and boots and T-shirts to fringed and sequined skirts and jackets of all colors and fabrics. The guys seemed to have more of a "look": the starched, long-sleeved, button-down shirts, neatly pressed blue jeans, shined boots, and cowboy hats that made a lot of them resemble . . . guess who?

The plaza outside the arena itself was like a country fair. Booths sponsored by radio stations were raffling off prizes. Children played games to win a stuffed toy or a water pistol. A huge inflated cow watched over the fun. Champion bull rider Ty Murray and *Playboy*'s Miss August, Melissa Wise, signed autographs. And down at the far end, folks lined up to pay fifty cents to see a huge snake.

The busiest booths by far were the ones where fans bought George Strait souvenirs. T-shirts commemorating the Fifth Annual George Strait Country Music Festival seemed to be the most popular, but other merchandise, including a fifteen-month George Strait calendar, was selling like crazy.

Inside the arena, where it was as cold as the inside of a refrigerator, lines formed quickly around the food and beer concession stands. By mid-afternoon, the audience was getting full and the arena was getting fuller as fans enjoyed the first few performers in the all-day concert event.

In San Antonio, Texas, as well as in many other parts of the American heartland, people tend to be amused by the idea of Garth Brooks and country music taking New York city by storm. Out in the rest of America, a nice guy in a cowboy hat singing about the real day-to-day joys and pains of life is as natural as the tall grasses growing out in the fields. It is also a tradition that goes back to the earliest days of the nation.

Garth Brooks is the flashy ambassador of country music. He's the high-flying, stage-leaping, trumpeting troubadour. His mega record sales and millions of devoted fans make him—and country music itself—a force that cannot be denied.

So let's see: Bob Wills, a man with Native American blood in his veins, unites the music of the country and the city, of black people and white people, of Mexican mariachis and German polka dancers, to create Western swing.

Merle Haggard and George Jones and Lefty Frizzell come in from the rural plains and Southern mountains singing real, down-home country music.

Western swing and traditional country music inspire George Strait to keep singing that music, even though he's told at first that he's "too country." George Strait keeps it country until the rest of the music business catches on that people really do want to hear these simple tales of real people trying to make it through the day and the night.

George Strait records "Unwound," which inspires a young pop- and rock-and-roll-loving musician, Garth Brooks, to take a look at country music. Garth Brooks takes country music to undreamed-of heights all over America, even to Central Park in New York City.

In New York, Garth Brooks sings with rock icon Billy Joel and folk/pop icon Don McLean. A month or so later, pop icon Sting sings in Nashville at the Country Music Awards.

Don't ya just love music?

Today, in San Antonio, the most influential country music artist of his generation is providing a great stage to those he considers some of the most important artists of the past year. Strait and his organization had selected these performers months and months before the show. Once again they showed how smart they were in picking acts whose stars had risen even higher by the end of the summer of 1997.

THE ALL-STAR LINEUP
AT THE GEORGE STRAIT
COUNTRY MUSIC FESTIVAL
SAN ANTONIO, LABOR DAY 1997

Here's what the stars have to say about their host.

LEE ANN WOMACK

"He has done more for this business than any artist in his generation. He made country music cool. He continues to do that today. Without Strait doing the music that he does and being the person that he is, I hate to think of where country music would be today."

MINDY McCREADY

"I've always loved him, even before I became successful, and thought it was appropriate that my first show with him was on Valentine's Day."

MARK CHESNUTT

"To me, George Strait has the perfect career. He's the country's top performer, yet he has time to hunt, ride, and be with his family. That's what I'm shooting for."

DEANA CARTER

"There are people in this business that are the real thing and people that aren't. George is the real thing."

TRACY LAWRENCE

"George Strait was, is, and will always be a big-time influence on me. I still love the man and his music."

LeANN RIMES

"I've grown up on his music and now, to be performing with him is an incredible thrill. . . . It would be hard to find any artist that George Strait hasn't had an influence on."

Lee Ann Womack performed her two big hits and a series of other songs that showcased her clear and delightful voice. The crowd loved her.

Then came Mindy McCready with a great set, including her hits "Ten Thousand Angels" and "Guys Do It All the Time." As the arena became even more crowded Strait's fellow Texan Mark Chesnutt took the stage and wowed the crowd with his new single, "Thank God for Believers," and other hits.

Deana Carter came onstage in the late afternoon, singing barefoot as she always does, with the great blue nail polish on her toenails a perfect match for her blue Gibson guitar. Turning up the heat with rockier renditions of songs from her debut CD, *Did I Shave My Legs For This?*, Carter was a real hit with "Strawberry Wine" and "We Danced Anyway," the two songs that will become her signatures for what looks to be a long career.

Tracy Lawrence, another of the talented "hat acts" that are grateful to George Strait for leading fans back to traditional country, sang a series of his high-charters, including "How a Cowgirl Says Goodbye" and "The Coast Is Clear."

Then, in the best position on the bill, second to closing, another Texas star, who some say is even bigger than country music itself, walked onto the stage in a simple blue dress with her blond hair framing her face. The amazing artist who had turned fifteen just a few days before held on to a wireless microphone and showed that in just over a year of touring she had learned to take command of even the biggest audiences.

Opening her set with her first number-one hit single, "One Way Ticket (Because I Can)," LeAnn Rimes went on to sing something old (the Patsy Montana classic "Cowboy's Sweetheart"), something new (her new hit single "How Do I Live?"), something borrowed (the Linda Rondstadt hit "You're No Good"), and something blue (her first big hit, "Blue"), and more in a set that was awesome.

Rimes left the stage at about 8:00 P.M. By this time, all the seats in the forty-seven-thousand-plus-capacity Alamodome were filled with fans who were breathless at all the music that had gone before.

Now they were wild with anticipation over what was to come.

After each of the different stars' shows at the George Strait Country Music Festival, stage crews came running out from behind the scenes to set up the stage for the next act. Each star and his or her band has different equipment, different monitors to help them hear the music onstage, and microphones in different positions on the stage.

While the audience was still excited over LeAnn Rimes, the crew for George Strait and the Ace in the Hole Band began setting the stage for the evening's headliners. First, all of Rimes's equipment came off the stage, leaving it almost empty. Then what seemed like miles of white material were spread across the entire stage. A riser platform about three quarters of the way back from the audience was also covered in this plain white fabric.

Now it was time for the large equipment to be moved—the instrument amplifiers for guitars, keyboards, and pedal steel guitars. Computer-controlled lighting was set up behind the stage.

The result was a starkly simple set. When the members of the stage crew stopped running in and out and the stage was again empty, the audience knew it was only a matter of time before the star and his band stepped out to entertain them.

Thirty minutes later, the stage was still empty. Now the wave had gone around the arena several times. The stomping and clapping and shouting and whistling were at a frenzied pitch. More than forty-seven thousand people, all of them George Strait fans, were as ready as they'd ever be to see his show.

"We want George, we want George!" After almost nine hours of being warmed up by the other terrific acts, even though the Alamodome was still cold, this crowd was HOT!

All it took was the dimming of the houselights and they were beyond help.

First, the Ace in the Hole Band came onstage and took their positions on the white platform. Now, everybody knows that a lead singer needs a band behind him, but few bands are as well known in their own right—or as well loved and respected—as the one and only Ace in the Hole Band. On their home turf in San Antone, the guys were greeted with the kinds of cheers usually reserved for the headliners.

The stage was bathed in light, from bright yellow to deep purple, from fiery red to cool blue. The effect of these colors on the white stage and platform was spectacular.

When the Ace in the Hole Band started playing "Deep in the Heart of Texas," every member of the audience, even those who had traveled from far outside the Texas borders, became an honorary citizen of the Lone Star State.

"Ladies and gentlemen," master of ceremonies Rick Gutierrez roared, "let's welcome Mr. George Strait!"

Out from behind the platform, wearing a crisp white shirt, a white hat, blue jeans, and a big belt buckle commemorating his annual rodeo event, the pride of San Antonio appeared in the spotlight. Right in the front among his most ardent fans were his father John Strait and his wife, Anna, along with George Jr., and Kara, George's brother's daughter. The huge video screens set up around the arena brought George Strait so close that each person felt he was singing to him or her alone.

The Bob Wills and the Texas Playboys classic "Take Me Back to Tulsa" turned the giant Alamodome into a Texas honky tonk. "Lovebug," a signature tune for Strait's hero George Jones, let the crowd know this would be a night of real country fare.

Strumming his Guild guitar, George Strait looked as happy and relaxed as any man would doing what he loves before a hometown crowd that loved him.

"Easy Come, Easy Go" and "Overnight Male" had the women in the audience melting as George Strait looked right into their eyes, smiling and flirting, and knowing full well the effect he was having on them.

The rainbow of lights continued to stream over the stage, first each color separately, then many colors at once. The songs the audience loved filled the arena up to its farthest corners. Now the star of the show wasn't the Ace in the Hole Band or even George Strait. The star of the show was the music.

After the first few songs, Strait thanked the audience for coming. A man of few words during his shows, he also asked whether the crowd agreed that "we had a great lineup this year."

The audience made it clear that they loved the lineup and loved hearing anything George Strait had to say.

"Here's a little 'pure country' music for you," he said, and that was all it took to put everyone on the edge of their seats.

Strait sang "When Did You Stop Loving Me?" with such a sweet, smiling, and flirtatious way about him that there was no way anyone would stop loving him. He and the Ace in the Hole Band performed a version of "Heartland" that split the difference between the movie's rock and simple country renditions. The rollicking "Where the Sidewalk Ends" got the crowd on its feet.

Men were jumping and stomping like they were at a Rolling Stones concert. And the women were steamed up and nearly sobbing as though it were 1966 and the Beatles were onstage.

All this hysteria in the audience and still, at the end of each song, all George Strait gave was a polite and modest bow accompanied by a quiet "thank you." That only served to get everyone even more shook up.

Introducing the members of the Ace in the Hole Band, Strait clearly enjoyed the applause his players were receiving. He's known to give them lots of time and space to show off their talents during the instrumental parts of the songs. "I've got a great band, so why not let 'em play," he says. "It's fun to get up there and not only play the records, but to do some other stuff as well, that's sometimes kind of off-the-wall, you know. I love the big-band sound."

Bob Wills used to do the same thing with his Texas Playboys.

THE PLATINUM TOUCH

Every single one of George Strait's albums has gone gold, which means it has sold more than half a million copies. After a while, the gold standard became almost too easy.

The next level of sales excitement is one million copies, a huge number, signified by the platinum standard. Double, triple, and quadruple platinum—two, three, and four *million* copies—are levels in the sales stratosphere that few albums ever reach.

Here's the list of George Strait albums that have climbed to those incredible heights.

PLATINUM

Strait from the Heart
Does Fort Worth Ever Cross Your Mind
Something Special
#7
Merry Christmas Strait to You
If You Ain't Lovin', You Ain't Livin'
Beyond the Blue Neon
Livin' It Up
The Chill of an Early Fall
Ten Strait Hits
Holding My Own
Lead On
Carrying Your Love with Me

DOUBLE PLATINUM

Easy Come, Easy Go
Blue Clear Sky

TRIPLE PLATINUM

Greatest Hits, Volume One
Greatest Hits, Volume Two

QUADRUPLE PLATINUM

Pure Country
Strait out of the Box

(By the way, only two George Strait albums
remain "just" Gold)
Strait Country
Right or Wrong

"I'd like to dedicate this to all the cowboys and
cowgirls who've been with me since the dance-
hall days," Strait said before starting "Amarillo by
Morning." When he got to the lyric ". . . up from
San Antone," the San Antonio Alamodome ex-
ploded in cheers.

Strait sang "Blue Clear Sky," "I Can Still Make
Cheyenne," "Carried Away," and "King of the
Mountain" with the joy and confidence of a man
at the top of his form. Mindful of all the young
fans who have recently discovered him, he sang
even more of his current songs, including "Carrying Your Love with Me," "Check Yes or No," "One
Night at a Time," and "Lead On."

For those who'd been with him from the start,
he sang "Unwound," the song that began the
journey from the half-empty Cheatham Street
Warehouse in San Marcos to the packed Alamodome in San Antone.

For fans old and young, longtime and new, he
closed the set with the song that always melts every
female heart in the room, "I Cross My Heart," playing up every nuance of that beautiful song.

Then George Strait said good night to the audience. He and the Ace in the Hole Band left the stage amid even more whooping and hollering.

The crowd had been in the Alamodome all day, enjoying the great music of fine country music acts topped off with a George Strait show they'd long remember. But they still weren't ready to let him go.

Carrying on until the lights dimmed one more time, the audience was rewarded for their hoarse throats and sore feet with the reappearance of the band, followed by George Strait. The band immediately launched into "The Fireman," the song about a loving guy who runs around town putting out old flames. Strait was smiling as broadly as he deserved to at the end of another season of touring, in a year where he'd topped the pop charts, in the town where he'd started it all.

The crowd was cheering like crazy as Strait sang his last line and left the stage as the band finished playing the song.

"This is where the cowboy rides away."

Just till next year. Strait's fans don't want that cowboy riding too far away.

Not long ago, a reporter asked George Strait what was next in his career.

"I'll probably stick around a while longer and play a few more dates," Strait said.

We'll count on it.

ACKNOWLEDGMENTS

Once again, I'd like to thank Cathy Repetti and everyone at Ballantine Books for being the best publishers I know.

One person at Ballantine who deserves special mention is Betsy Flagler. I know I'm not the only author who has benefited from her professional input and support.

Thanks again to the executives at Entertainment Management Group. Ira Fraitag, who knows more about music than anyone I know, has taught me that there are really only two kinds of music: good music and bad music. Sol Saffian's expert knowledge of the music business is exceeded only by his great sense of humor.

The country music biographies of Tom Carter have inspired me over the years and I thank him.

I enjoyed Jimmy Bowen's unabashed look at the country music business in his book, _Rough Mix_, and I know all of George Strait's fans join me in thanking him for telling George to make music his way.

Hats off to the superbly talented songwriters who create the lyrics and sounds that make the music business possible in the first place. The stories they tell in three minutes are the envy of all writers.

Judith Mandelbaum at Burrelle's Business Research Center again proved herself invaluable.

Ronnie Pugh and Kent Henderson of the Country Music Foundation Library and Media Center were unfailingly helpful in guiding me to the resources I needed to complete my research.

Mark Ford of the Nashville Songwriters Association International opened his office and his files to me, for which I am very grateful.

Working on a creative project in Nashville, Tennessee, is a great experience. As a relative newcomer to Music City, I am truly appreciative of the courtesy, hospitality, and generosity of all the people who have made this job easier for me.

All of my friends and family give me deeply appreciated support in my life and work. I'd like to give particular thanks to my friend and colleague Marilyn J. Abraham for encouraging me to write country music biographies.

Last, but never least, my husband, Ira Fraitag, is the smartest, funniest, and kindest person I know. And he's one hell of a music maker himself.

The dazzling rise of a young country star . . .

DREAM COME TRUE
The LeAnn Rimes Story
by Jo Sgammato

LeAnn Rimes, owner of a huge, God-given voice, was born knowing what she wanted to do and sang with assurance when she was just a toddler. She burst onto the country-music scene with one great song, "Blue," an old-fashioned ballad originally written for the legendary Patsy Cline. Her album of the same name hit the charts at number one, and LeAnn became one of the biggest entertainment stories of the year.

But as young as she was, this overnight sensation was years in the making. Here is the heartwarming story of LeAnn Rimes and her parents, Belinda and Wilbur Rimes, an American family who made a DREAM COME TRUE.

Lorrie Morgan was born to be
a country-western music star.

In FOREVER YOURS, FAITHFULLY,
she tells her tempestuous story of sweet
triumph and bitter tragedy.
From her childhood as a Nashville blueblood,
performing at the Grand Ole Opry at the tender
age of eleven, to her turbulent,
star-crossed love affair with Keith Whitley,
a bluegrass legend she loved passionately
but could not save from his personal demons,
to her rise to superstardom,
she lays bare all the secrets and great passions
of a life lived to the fullest.

And her story would not be complete without
the music that has been her lifeline.

**A special four-song CD of
never-before-released material,
featuring a duet with Keith Whitley,
is included with this hardcover.**

FOREVER YOURS, FAITHFULLY
by Lorrie Morgan

Published by Ballantine Books.
Available wherever books are sold.

"Outrageous, breathless, voluble, fast-moving, funny . . . and always mercilessly candid."
—*Chicago Tribune*

LOVE CAN BUILD A BRIDGE
by Naomi Judd
with Bud Schaetzle

For eight glorious years, Naomi Judd and daughter Wynonna lived the American dream. Signed by RCA in 1983 after a rare live audition, they became country music's most honored and successful women— winning six Grammys and selling more than fifteen million albums.

Then Naomi learned she had a life-threatening liver disease. Forced to retire, the Judds went on a farewell tour that broke America's heart and ended one of the most beloved country-music acts of all time.

But Naomi never gave up. And here is her story: the true story of a mother and daughter who sang like angels and fought like devils, but loved each other through struggle, tragedy, and triumph.